The Picador Book of

Wedding Poems

PETER FORBES is the editor of the anthologies *Scanning the Century: The Penguin Book of the Twentieth Century in Poetry* (Penguin, 2000) and *We Have Come Through: 100 Poems Celebrating Courage in Overcoming Depression and Trauma* (Bloodaxe/Survivors' Poetry, 2003). He edited the Poetry Society's magazine *Poetry Review* from 1986 to 2002, and is the author of *The Gecko's Foot: How Scientists are Taking a Leaf from Nature's Book*. His cultural history of camouflage and mimicry in nature, art and warfare, *Dazzled and Deceived: Mimicry and Camouflage* (Yale University Press), won the 2011 Warwick Prize for Writing.

The Picador Book of

Wedding Poems

EDITED BY

Peter Forbes

PICADOR

First published 2012 by Picador
an imprint of Pan Macmillan, a division of Macmillan Publishers Limited
Pan Macmillan, 20 New Wharf Road, London N1 9RR
Basingstoke and Oxford
Associated companies throughout the world
www.panmacmillan.com

ISBN 978-0-330-45686-9

A version of this book was originally published by Picador in 2004 as
All the Poems You Need to Say I Do.

The acknowledgements on pages xi–xiii constitute an extension of
this copyright page.

3 5 7 9 8 6 4 2

A CIP catalogue record for this book is available from
the British Library.

Printed and bound by CPI Group (UK) Ltd, Croydon, CR0 4YY

Visit **www.picador.com** to read more about all our books
and to buy them. You will also find features, author interviews and
news of any author events, and you can sign up for e-newsletters
so that you're always first to hear about our new releases.

Contents

Tests, Trials and Torments

Time Was Away

Acknowledgements

Gillian Allnutt, 'Ode', by permission of the author; W. H. Auden, 'Alone', copyright © 1976, 1991, The Estate of W. H. Auden; Patricia Beer, 'The Faithful Wife', from *Collected Poems*, 1990, published by Carcanet Press Limited; John Betjeman, 'In a Bath Teashop', copyright © John Betjeman by permission of The Estate of John Betjeman; Robert Bly, 'Rainy September' from *Loving a Woman in Two Worlds* by Robert Bly. Copyright © 1985 by Robert Bly. Reprinted by permission of Georges Borchardt, Inc., for Robert Bly; Alison Brackenbury, 'Hawthorn', from *Selected Poems*, 1991, published by Carcanet Press Limited; Eleanor Brown, from 'Fifty Sonnets', nos III and IX, from *Maiden Speech* (Bloodaxe Books, 1996); Kate Clanchy, 'For a Wedding', by permission of Macmillan Publishers Ltd; Austin Clarke, 'The Planter's Daughter', by permission of R. Dardis Clarke, 17 Oscar Square, Dublin 8, from Austin Clarke, *Collected Poems*, edited by R. Dardis Clarke, published by Carcanet / The Bridge Press (2008); Julia Copus, 'In Defence of Adultery', from *In Defence of Adultery* (Bloodaxe Books, 2003); Gregory Corso, 'Marriage' by Gregory Corso, from *The Happy Birthday of Death*, copyright © 1960 by New Directions Publishing Corp. Reprinted by permission of New Directions Publishing Corp.; 'i carry your heart with me(i carry it in my heart)'. Copyright 1952, © 1980, 1991 by the Trustees for the E. E. Cummings Trust, from *Complete Poems: 1904–1962* by E. E. Cummings, edited by George J. Firmage. Used by permission of Liveright Publishing Corporation; Kamala Das, 'The Looking Glass', by permission of the author; Carol Ann Duffy, 'White Writing', by permission of Macmillan Publishers Ltd; Bob Dylan, 'Boots of Spanish Leather', by permission of Bob Dylan and Special Rider Music; 'Atlas', from *New and Collected Poems*, Enitharmon Press, 2010, by permission of the library executor;

Elizabeth Garrett, 'Epithalamium', by permission of the author; Atar Hadari, 'Life is Very Long', by permission of the author; Mark Halliday, 'the Beloved', by permission of the author; Sophie Hannah, 'Over and Elm and I', from *Leaving You and Leaving You*, 1999, published by Carcanet Press Limited, and 'Match', from *First of the Last Chances*, 2003, published by Carcanet Press Limited; Rita Ann Higgins, 'The Did-You-Come-Yets of the Western World', from *Throw in the Vowels: New & Selected Poems* (Bloodaxe Books, 2005); Jane Holland, 'They Are a Tableau at the Kissing-Gate', by permission of the author; Elizabeth Jennings, 'Delay', from *New Collected Poems*, 2002, published by Carcanet Press Limited; Brian Jones, 'Husband to Wife: Party-Going', by permission of Noëlle Soret-Jones; P. J. Kavanagh, extract from 'The Perfect Stranger', from *The Perfect Stranger*, 1966, by permission of Carcanet Press Limited; Philip Larkin, 'Waiting for breakfast, while she brushed her hair', from *Collected Poems* by Philip Larkin, published by Faber and Faber Ltd, and with permission from The Society of Authors, on behalf of the Estate of Philip Larkin; D. H. Lawrence, 'Fidelity', reproduced by permission of Pollinger Limited and The Estate of Frieda Lawrence Ravagli; Louis MacNeice, 'Meeting Point', from *Collected Poems*, 1966, published by Faber and Faber Ltd; Michael Levene, 'Hymn to Aphrodite', by permission of the author; Norman MacCaig, 'True Ways of Knowing', from *The Poems of Norman MacCaig* by Norman MacCaig is reproduced by permission of Polygon, an imprint of Birlinn Ltd (www.birlinn.co.uk); Roger McGough, 'At Lunchtime' by Roger McGough from *The Mersey Sound* (© Roger McGough, 1967) is printed by permission of United Agents (www.unitedagents.co.uk) on behalf of Roger McGough; Glyn Maxwell, 'Stargazing', from *Boys at Twilight: New & Selected Poems* (Bloodaxe Books, 2000) and from *The Boys at Twilight: Poems 1990–1995* by Glyn Maxwell. Copyright © 1990, 1992, 2000 by Glyn Maxwell. Reprinted by permission of Houghton Mifflin Harcourt

Introduction

It's no secret that love is the poets' favourite subject, and although writing a sonnet may not be the obvious way to the beloved's heart that it was in Shakespeare's day, poetry retains a talismanic quality for lovers.

The path of love never ran smooth and in this book the process has three stations of the heart: the kindling of desire, the various tests, trials and torments that decide whether fulfilment will be reached, and, finally, that realm in which something like a civilization is founded.

If you're in the first throes of a new excitement, or need to put a new relationship to the test, or put a failure behind you, or have reached the point of the great affirmation, you'll find a poem here for the occasion.

First Sight of Her and After

Conviction (iv)

I like to get off with people,
I like to lie in their arms,
I like to be held and tightly kissed,
Safe from all alarms.

I like to laugh and be happy
With a beautiful beautiful kiss,
I tell you, in all the world
There is no bliss like this.

STEVIE SMITH

Love: Beginnings

They're at that stage where so much desire streams
    between them, so much frank need and want,
so much absorption in the other and the self and the self-
    admiring entity and unity they make –
her mouth so full, breast so lifted, head thrown back so far
    in her laughter at his laughter,
he so solid, planted, oaky, firm, so resonantly factual in the
    headiness of being craved so,
she almost wreathed upon him as they intertwine again,
    touch again, cheek, lip, shoulder, brow,
every glance moving toward the sexual, every glance away
    soaring back in flame into the sexual –
that just to watch them is to feel again that hitching in the
    groin, that filling of the heart,
the old, sore heart, the battered, foundered, faithful heart,
    snorting again, stamping in its stall.

C. K. Williams

Wild Nights

Wild nights! Wild nights!
Were I with thee,
Wild nights should be
Our luxury!

Futile the winds
To a heart in port, –
Done with the compass,
Done with the chart.

Rowing in Eden!
Ah! the sea!
Might I but moor
To-night in thee!

EMILY DICKINSON

The Mower to the Glo-Worms

Ye living lamps, by whose dear light
The nightingale does sit so late,
And studying all the summer-night,
Her matchless songs does meditate;

Ye country comets, that portend
No war, nor prince's funeral,
Shining unto no higher end
Then to presage the grasses' fall;

Ye glo-worms, whose officious flame
To wandering mowers shows the way,
That in the night have lost their aim,
And after foolish fires do stray;

Your courteous lights in vain you waste,
Since *Juliana* here is come,
For she my mind hath so displaced
That I shall never find my home.

ANDREW MARVELL

from *The Bothie of Tober-Na-Vuolich*

I have been kissed before, she added, blushing slightly,
I have been kissed more than once by Donald my cousin,
    and others;
It is the way of the lads, and I make up my mind not to
    mind it;
But Mr Philip, last night, and from you, it was different
    quite, Sir.
When I think of all that, I am shocked and terrified at it.
Yes, it is dreadful to me.
                            She paused, but quickly continued,
Smiling almost fiercely, continued, looking upward.
You are too strong, you see, Mr Philip! just like the sea
    there,
Which *will* come, through the straits and all between the
    mountains,
Forcing its great strong tide into every nook and inlet,
Getting far in, up the quiet stream of sweet inland water,
Sucking it up, and stopping it, turning it, driving it
    backward,
Quite preventing its own quiet running: and then, soon
    after,
Back it goes off, leaving weeds on the shore, and wrack
    and uncleanness:
And the poor burn in the glen tries again its peaceful
    running,
But it is brackish and tainted, and all its banks in disorder.
That was what I dreamt all last night. I was the burnie,

Trying to get along through the tyrannous brine, and
    could not;
I was confined and squeezed in the coils of the great salt
    tide, that
Would mix-in itself with me, and change me; I felt myself
    changing;
And I struggled, and screamed, I believe, in my dream. It
    was dreadful.
You are too strong, Mr Philip! I am but a poor slender
    burnie,
Used to the glens and the rocks, the rowan and birch of
    the woodies,
Quite unused to the great salt sea; quite afraid and
    unwilling.

ARTHUR HUGH CLOUGH

In Defence of Adultery

We don't fall in love: it rises through us
the way that certain music does –
whether a symphony or ballad –
and it is sepia-coloured,
like spilt tea that inches up
the tiny tube-like gaps inside
a cube of sugar lying by a cup.
Yes, love's like that: just when we least
needed or expected it
a part of us dips into it
by chance or mishap and it seeps
through our capillaries, it clings
inside the chambers of the heart.
We're victims, we say: mere vessels,
drinking the vanilla scent
of this one's skin, the lustre
of another's eyes so skilfully
darkened with bistre. And whatever
damage might result we're not
to blame for it: love is an autocrat
and won't be disobeyed.
Sometimes we manage
to convince ourselves of that.

JULIA COPUS

9

It Was a Quiet Way

It was a quiet way –
He asked if I was his –
I made no answer of the Tongue
But answer of the Eyes –
And then He bore me on.
Before this mortal noise
With swiftness, as of Chariots.
And distance, as of Wheels.
The World did drop away
As Acres from the feet
Of one that leaneth from Balloon
Upon an Ether street.
The Gulf behind was not,
The Continents were new –
Eternity it was before
Eternity was due.
No seasons were to us –
That was not Night nor Morn –
But Sunrise stopped upon the place
And fastened it in Dawn.

EMILY DICKINSON

from Fifty Sonnets

III

When Dante first saw Beatrice, she wore
a red dress – probably not much like mine.
Allowing, though, for accident (design,
and taste, and length, and Lycra), what he saw
was more or less what you saw on the night
when I decided you were mine. My dress
was red in its intent and – more or less –
red in its consequence. And I was right
to wear it, and play 'queen' with those poor boys
who didn't know quite what was going on,
and deferentially provided noise
of admiration and desire. These gone,
certain of these, and certain of your bed,
we left; and the rest is taken as read.

ELEANOR BROWN

The Planter's Daughter

When night stirred at sea
And the fire brought a crowd in,
They say that her beauty
Was music in mouth
And few in the candlelight
Thought her too proud,
For the house of the planter
Is known by the trees.

Men that had seen her
Drank deep and were silent,
The women were speaking
Wherever she went –
As a bell that is rung
Or a wonder told shyly,
And O she was the Sunday
In every week.

AUSTIN CLARKE

First Sight of Her and After

A day is drawing to its fall
    I had not dreamed to see;
The first of many to enthrall
    My spirit, will it be?
Or is this eve the end of all
    Such new delight for me?

I journey home: the pattern grows
    Of moonshades on the way:
'Soon the first quarter, I suppose,'
    Sky-glancing travellers say;
I realize that it, for those,
    Has been a common day.

THOMAS HARDY

In Three Days

So, I shall see her in three days
And just one night, but nights are short,
Then two long hours, and that is morn.
See how I come, unchanged, unworn!
Feel, where my life broke off from thine,
How fresh the splinters keep and fine, –
Only a touch and we combine!

Too long, this time of year, the days!
But nights, at least the nights are short.
As night shows where her one moon is,
A hand's-breadth of pure light and bliss,
So life's night gives my lady birth
And my eyes hold her! What is worth
The rest of heaven, the rest of earth?

O loaded curls, release your store
Of warmth and scent, as once before
The tingling hair did, lights and darks
Outbreaking into fairy sparks,
When under curl and curl I pried
After the warmth and scent inside,
Thro' lights and darks how manifold –
The dark inspired, the light controlled!
As early Art embrowns the gold.

What great fear, should one say, 'Three days
'That change the world might change as well
'Your fortune; and if joy delays,
'Be happy that no worse befell!'
What small fear, if another says,
'Three days and one short night beside
'May throw no shadow on your ways;
'But years must teem with change untried,
'With chance not easily defied,
'With an end somewhere undescried.'
No fear! – or if a fear be born
This minute, it dies out in scorn.
Fear? I shall see her in three days
And one night, now the nights are short,
Then just two hours, and that is morn.

ROBERT BROWNING

Meeting at Night

The grey sea and the long black land,
And the yellow half-moon large and low;
And the startled little waves that leap
In fiery ringlets from their sleep,
As I gain the cove with pushing prow,
And quench its speed i' the slushy sand.

Then a mile of warm sea-scented beach;
Three fields to cross till a farm appears;
A tap at the pane, the quick sharp scratch
And blue spurt of a lighted match,
And a voice less loud, thro' its joys and fears,
Than the two hearts beating each to each!

ROBERT BROWNING

'If you were coming in the fall'

If you were coming in the fall,
I'd brush the summer by
With half a smile and half a spurn,
As housewives do a fly.

If I could see you in a year,
I'd wind the months in balls,
And put them each in separate drawers,
Until their time befalls.

If only centuries delayed,
I'd count them on my hand,
Subtracting till my fingers dropped
Into Van Diemen's land.

If certain, when this life was out,
That yours and mine should be,
I'd toss it yonder like a rind,
And taste eternity.

But now, all ignorant of the length
Of time's uncertain wing,
It goads me, like the goblin bee,
That will not state its sting.

EMILY DICKINSON

The Bait

Come live with me, and be my love,
And we will some new pleasures prove
Of golden sands and crystal brooks,
With silken lines and silver hooks.

There will the river whispering run
Warmed by thy eyes, more than the sun.
And there the'enamoured fish will stay,
Begging themselves they may betray.

When thou wilt swim in that live bath,
Each fish, which every channel hath,
Will amorously to thee swim,
Gladder to catch thee, than thou him.

If thou, to be so seen, be'st loth,
By sun, or moon, thou darkenest both,
And if myself have leave to see,
I need not their light, having thee.

Let others freeze with angling reeds,
And cut their legs with shells and weeds,
Or treacherously poor fish beset,
With strangling snare or windowy net:

Let coarse bold hands, from slimy nest
The bedded fish in banks out-wrest,

Or curious traitors, sleavesilk flies
Bewitch poor fishes' wandering eyes.

For thee, thou need'st no such deceit,
For thou thyself art thine own bait:
That fish, that is not catched thereby,
Alas, is wiser far than I.

JOHN DONNE

The Passionate Shepherd to His Love

Come live with me, and be my love,
And we will all the pleasures prove,
That valleys, groves, hills and fields,
Woods, or steepy mountain yields.

And we will sit upon the rocks,
Seeing the shepherds feed their flocks
By shallow rivers, to whose falls
Melodious birds sing madrigals.

And I will make thee beds of roses,
And a thousand fragrant posies,
A cap of flowers and a kirtle
Embroidered all with leaves of myrtle.

A gown made of the finest wool
Which from our pretty lambs we pull,
Fair lined slippers for the cold,
With buckles of the purest gold;

A belt of straw and ivy-buds,
With coral clasps and amber studs,
And if these pleasures may thee move,
Come live with me, and be my love.

The shepherd swains shall dance and sing
For thy delight each May-morning,
If these delights thy mind may move;
Then live with me, and be my love.

CHRISTOPHER MARLOWE

My Sweetest Lesbia

My sweetest Lesbia, let us live and love;
And, though the sager sort our deeds reprove,
Let us not weigh them. Heaven's great lamps do dive
Into their west, and straight again revive.
But soon as once set is our little light,
Then must we sleep one ever-during night.

If all would lead their lives in love like me,
Then bloody swords and armour should not be;
No drum nor trumpet peaceful sleeps should move,
Unless alarm came from the camp of Love.
But fools do live and waste their little light,
And seek with pain their ever-during night.

When timely death my life and fortune ends,
Let not my hearse be vexed with mourning friends
But let all lovers, rich in triumph, come
And with sweet pastimes grace my happy tomb.
And, Lesbia, close up thou my little light,
And crown with love my ever-during night.

THOMAS CAMPION

Ode

To depict a (bicycle), you must first come to love (it).
Alexander Blok

I swear by every rule in the bicycle
owner's manual

that I love you, I, who have repeatedly,
painstakingly,

with accompanying declaration of despair,
tried to repair

you, to patch things up,
to maintain a workable relationship.

I have spent sleepless nights
in pondering your parts – those private

and those that all who walk the street
may look at –

wondering what makes you tick
over smoothly, or squeak.

my trusty steed,
my rusty three-speed,

I would feed you the best oats
if oats

were applicable.
Only linseed oil

will do
to nourish you.

I want
so much to paint

you,
midnight blue

mudgutter black
and standing as you do, ironic

at the rail
provided by the Council –

beautiful
the sun caught in your back wheel –

or at home in the hall, remarkable
among other bicycles,

your handlebars erect.
Allow me to depict

you thus. And though I can't do justice
to your true opinion of the surface

of the road –
put into words

the nice distinctions that you make
among the different sorts of tarmac –

still I'd like to set the record of our travels straight.
I'd have you know that

not with three-in-one
but with my own

heart's
spittle I anoint your moving parts.

GILLIAN ALLNUTT

The Fair Singer

To make a final conquest of all me,
Love did compose so sweet an enemy,
In whom both beauties to my death agree,
Joining themselves in fatal harmony,
That, while she with her eyes my heart does bind,
She with her voice might captivate my mind.

I could have fled from one but singly fair;
My disentangled soul itself might save.
Breaking the curled trammels of her hair;
But how should I avoid to be her slave,
Whose subtle art invisibly can wreath
My fetters of the very air I breathe?

It had been easy fighting in some plain,
Where victory might hang in equal choice,
But all resistance against her is vain
Who has the advantage both of eyes and voice,
And all my forces needs must be undone
She having gained both the wind and sun.

ANDREW MARVELL

Wishes: To His (Supposed) Mistress

Whoe'er she be,
That not impossible she
That shall command my heart and me;

Where'er she lie,
Locked up from mortal eye
In shady leaves of destiny

Till that ripe birth
Of studied fate stand forth,
And teach her fair steps to our Earth;

Till that divine
Idea take a shrine
Of crystal flesh, through which to shine;

Meet you her, my wishes,
Bespeak her to my blisses,
And be ye called my absent kisses.

I wish her beauty
That owes not all his duty
To gaudy tire or glistering shoe-tie;

Something more than
Taffeta or tissue can,
Or rampant feather, or rich fan;

More than the spoil
Of shop, or silkworm's toil,
Or a bought blush, or a set smile;

A face that's best
By its own beauty dressed,
And can alone command the rest;

A face made up
Out of no other shop
Than what nature's white hand sets ope;

A cheek where youth
And blood, with pen of truth,
Write what the reader sweetly ru'th;

A cheek where grows
More than a morning rose:
Which to no box his being owes;

Lips where all day
A lover's kiss may play,
Yet carry nothing thence away;

Looks that oppress
Their richest tires, but dress
And clothe their simplest nakedness;

Eyes that displaces
The neighbour diamond, and outfaces
The sunshine by their own sweet graces;

Tresses that wear
Jewels but to declare
How much themselves more precious are;

Whose native ray
Can tame the wanton day
Of gems, that in their bright shades play –

Each ruby there,
Or pearl that dare appear,
Be its own blush, be its own tear;

A well-tamed heart,
For whose more noble smart
Love may be long choosing a dart;

Eyes that bestow
Full quivers on love's bow,
Yet pay less arrows than they owe;

Smiles that can warm
The blood, yet teach a charm,
That chastity shall take no harm;

Blushes that bin
The burnish of no sin,
Nor flames of aught too hot within;

Joys that confess
Virtue their mistress,
And have no other head to dress;

Fears, fond and flight
As the coy bride's, when night
First does the longing lover right;

Tears quickly fled
And vain, as those are shed
For a dying maidenhead;

Days that need borrow
No part of their good morrow
From a forespent night of sorrow;

Days that, in spite
Of darkness, by the light
Of a clear mind are day all night;

Nights sweet as they,
Made short by lover's play
Yet long by the absence of the day;

Life that dares send
A challenge to his end,
And, when it comes, say, 'Welcome, friend.'

Sydnaean showers
Of sweet discourse, whose powers
Can crown old winter's head with flowers;

Soft silken hours,
Open suns, shady bowers;
'Bove all, nothing within that lours;

Whate'er delight
Can make day's forehead bright,
Or give down to the wings of night;

In her whole frame
Have nature all the name,
Art and ornament the shame;

Her flattery,
Picture and poesy:
Her counsel her own virtue be;

I wish her store
Of worth may leave her poor
Of wishes; and I wish – no more.

Now if time knows
That her whose radiant brows
Weave them a garland of my vows;

Her whose just bays
My future hopes can raise,
A trophy to her present praise;

Her that dares be
What these lines wish to see:
I seek no further: it is she.

'Tis she, and here
Lo! I unclothe and clear
My wishes' cloudy character.

May she enjoy it
Whose merit dare apply it,
But modesty dares still deny it.

Such worth as this is
Shall fix my flying wishes,
And determine them to kisses.

Let her full glory,
My fancies, fly before ye:
Be ye my fictions, but her story.

RICHARD CRASHAW

To His Coy Mistress

Had we but world enough, and time,
This coyness, Lady, were no crime.
We would sit down, and think which way
To walk, and pass our long love's day.
Thou by the Indian Ganges' side
Shouldst rubies find: I by the tide
Of Humber would complain. I would
Love you ten years before the Flood:
And you should, if you please, refuse
Till the conversion of the Jews.
My vegetable love should grow
Vaster than empires, and more slow.
An hundred years should go to praise
Thine eyes, and on thy forehead gaze.
Two hundred to adore each breast;
    But thirty thousand to the rest.
An age at least to every part,
And the last age should show your heart:
For, Lady, you deserve this state;
Nor would I love at lower rate.
    But at my back I always hear
Time's wingèd chariot hurrying near;
And yonder all before us lie
Deserts of vast eternity.
Thy beauty shall no more be found;
Nor, in thy marble vault, shall sound
My echoing song: then worms shall try
That long-preserved virginity:

And your quaint honour turn to dust;
And into ashes all my lust.
The grave's a fine and private place,
But none, I think, do there embrace.

Now, therefore, while the youthful glue
Sits on thy skin like morning dew,
And while thy willing soul transpires
At every pore with instant fires,
Now let us sport us while we may;
And now, like amorous birds of prey,
Rather at once our time devour,
Than languish in his slow-chapped power.
Let us roll all our strength, and all
Our sweetness, up into one ball:
And tear our pleasures with rough strife
Thorough the iron gates of life.
Thus, though we cannot make our sun
Stand still, yet we will make him run.

ANDREW MARVELL

The Sun Rising

Busy old fool, unruly sun,
    Why dost thou thus
Through windows and through curtains call on us?
Must to thy motions lovers' seasons run?
    Saucy pedantic wretch, go chide
    Late schoolboys and sour prentices;
Go tell court huntsmen that the king will ride;
    Call country ants to harvest offices:
Love, all alike, no season knows, nor clime,
Nor hours, days, months, which are the rags of time.

Thy beams, so reverend and strong
    Why shouldst thou think?
I could eclipse and cloud them with a wink,
But that I would not lose her sight so long:
    If her eyes have not blinded thine,
    Look, and tomorrow late tell me
Whether both th' Indias of spice and mine
Be where thou leftst them, or lie here with me.
Ask for those kings whom thou sawst yesterday.
And thou shalt hear, all here in one bed lay.

She's all states, and all princes, I;
    Nothing else is.
Princes do but play us; compared to this,
All honour's mimic; all wealth alchemy.
    Thou, sun, art half as happy as we,
    In that the world's contracted thus;

Thine age asks ease, and since thy duties be
To warm the world, that's done in warming us.
Shine here to us, and thou art everywhere:
This bed thy centre is, these walls, thy sphere.

JOHN DONNE

from The Hunting of Cupid

What thing is love? for, well I wot, love is a thing.
It is a prick, it is a sting,
It is a pretty pretty thing;
It is a fire, it is a coal,
Whose flame creeps in at every hole;
And as my wit doth best devise,
Love's dwelling is in ladies' eyes:
From whence do glance love's piercing darts
That make such holes into our hearts;
And all the world herein accord
Love is a great and mighty lord,
And when he list to mount so high,
With Venus he in heaven doth lie,
And evermore hath been a god
Since Mars and she played even and odd.

GEORGE PEELE

Poet, Lover, Birdwatcher

To force the pace and never to be still
Is not the way of those who study birds
Or women. The best poets wait for words.
The hunt is not an exercise of will
But patient love relaxing on a hill
To note the movement of a timid wing;
Until the one who knows that she is loved
No longer waits but risks surrendering –
In this the poet finds his moral proved,
Who never spoke before his spirit moved.

The slow movement seems, somehow, to say
    much more.
To watch the rarer birds, you have to go
Along deserted lanes and where the rivers flow
In silence near the source, or by a shore
Remote and thorny like the heart's dark floor.
And there the women slowly turn around,
Not only flesh and bone but myths of light
With darkness at the core, and sense is found
By poets lost in crooked, restless flight,
The deaf can hear, the blind recover sight.

NISSIM EZEKIEL

To His Mistress Going to Bed

Come, Madam, come, all rest my powers defy,
Until I labour, I in labour lie.
The foe oft-times having the foe in sight,
Is tired with standing though they never fight.
Off with that girdle, like heaven's zone glistering,
But a far fairer world encompassing.
Unpin that spangled breastplate which you wear,
That th'eyes of busy fools may be stopped there.
Unlace yourself, for that harmonious chime
Tells me from you, that now 'tis your bed time.
Off with that happy busk, which I envy,
That still can be, and still can stand so nigh.
Your gown going off, such beauteous state reveals,
As when from flowery meads th'hill's shadow steals.
Off with that wiry coronet and show
The hairy diadem which on you doth grow;
Now off with those shoes, and then safely tread
In this love's hallowed temple, this soft bed.
In such white robes heaven's angels used to be
Received by men; thou angel bring'st with thee
A heaven like Mahomet's paradise; and though
Ill spirits walk in white, we easily know
By this these angels from an evil sprite:
Those set our hairs, but these our flesh upright.
    Licence my roving hands, and let them go
Before, behind, between, above, below.
O my America, my new found land,
My kingdom, safeliest when with one man manned,

My mine of precious stones, my empery,
How blessed am I in this discovering thee!
To enter in these bonds, is to be free;
Then where my hand is set, my seal shall be.
    Full nakedness, all joys are due to thee.
As souls unbodied, bodies unclothed must be,
To taste whole joys. Gems which you women use
Are like Atlanta's balls, cast in men's views,
That when a fool's eye lighteth on a gem,
His earthly soul may covet theirs, not them.
Like pictures, or like books' gay coverings made
For laymen, are all women thus arrayed;
Themselves are mystic books, which only we
Whom their imputed grace will dignify
Must see revealed. Then since I may know,
As liberally, as to a midwife, show
Thyself: cast all, yea, this white linen hence,
Here is no penance, much less innocence.
    To teach thee, I am naked first, why then
What needst thou have more covering than a man.

JOHN DONNE

The Tantric Master

For I shall consider his beautiful navel firstly
– an altar! – whereat I've often offered flowers,
the yellow buttercup especially, a monstrance I can elevate
to the memory of his mother who surely taught him to
        pet.
And honeysuckle and meadowsweet and the wild dog
        rose:
one for its scent, one for its sound, and one for the tone of
        his skin
that is all petal to me.

                For I shall consider
secondly each individuated pore of his entire body
and consider each at length having nothing better
to do with my time, and each being a universe unto itself.
This I call rapture.

                And thirdly, to make no bones
about it, being the crux, the hardest part of the matter,
I shall consider his noble and magical wand. He do good
business throughout the night with it. He enchant,
and spellbind and wind me round his little finger;
or, on a moony night in April, even his little toe.

Which brings me to his nails: he keepeth that trim and
        smooth
the better to pleasure me. So subtle his touch I can feel

the very whorls of his fingerprints and could reconstruct
    from memory
his mark on my breast. Each ridge the high mountain,
each trough the deep canyon, unfathomable;
but I, having buckets of time, do fathom, do fathom.

For I shall consider the mesmeric draw of his nipples,
like tribal erections on the broad plain of his chest,
megalithic power spots when I lay my hot cheek
on the cool of his belly and sight through the meadows
and the distant forests the trajectory of sun and other
    stars.

His mouth, I won't go into, being all cliché in the face
    of it,
except to say the dip of his lip is most suited to suction
    and friction,
and other words ending in tion, tion, tion, which come to
    think of it
when I'm in the grip of it, is exactly how I make sweet
    moan.

You can keep your third eyes and your orbs sanctimonious
the opening of which my Master believes *is* the point.
He says I'm a natural and ultimate enlightenment a mere
    question of time.
But in patient devotion I'll admit to deficiency. The theory
    of being –
not a patch on just being. Yap I distrust! Show me.
Don't tell me the way. The right place for talk of this ilk

is not during, not after, and foretalk will get you nowhere
    at all.
The best that I hope for in our daily instructions
is the lull between breaths, spent and near pacified.

PAULA MEEHAN

The Water Bearer

When I walk in the streets at night
Following the lamplight to where it falls
Exhausted in my head, some girl
Still carries my love on her shoulders through
   the crowd
Which sometimes offers up her face to me
Like a book which flickers shut again.

So long I have tried to touch that face
When it drifts for a moment near me on the tide.
So many times I have seen it
Sucked back into the sea
Of all such nights I follow down like stones
To where they lie unfound, unfathomable.

When I wake in the morning, far from her,
This girl, wherever she is sleeping, wakes with me
And takes up the weight of my love for her,
Carrying it back into the world of absences
Where I see her walking alone in the streets
Cursed as she is with being mine.

For her shoulders that are always disappearing
Into the heart of her own searching
Look so calm and beautiful despite it all

That I wait impatiently for the sight of her
Passing again so sweetly through my life
As if she carried water from a well.

HUGO WILLIAMS

Leaning into the Afternoons

Leaning into the afternoons I cast my sad nets
towards your oceanic eyes.

There in the highest blaze my solitude lengthens
    and flames,
its arms turning like a drowning man's.

I send out red signals across your absent eyes
that wave like the sea or the beach by a lighthouse.

You keep only darkness, my distant female,
from your regard sometimes the coast of dread
    emerges.

Leaning into the afternoons I fling my sad nets
to that sea that is thrashed by your oceanic eyes.

The birds of night peck at the first stars
that flash like my soul when I love you.

The night gallops on its shadowy mare
shedding blue tassels over the land.

PABLO NERUDA
Translated by W. S. Merwin

At Lunchtime – A Story of Love

When the bus stopped suddenly
to avoid damaging
a mother and child in the road,
the younglady in the green hat sitting opposite,
was thrown across me,
and not being one to miss an opportunity
i started to make love.

At first, she resisted,
saying that it was too early in the morning,
and too soon after breakfast,
and anyway, she found me repulsive.
But when i explained
that this being a nuclearage
the world was going to end at lunchtime,
she took off her green hat,
put her busticket into her pocket
and joined in the exercise.

The buspeople,
and there were many of them,
were shockedandsurprised,
and amusedandannoyed.
But when word got around
that the world was going to end at lunchtime,
they put their pride in their pockets
with their bustickets
and made love one with the other.

And even the busconductor,
feeling left out,
climbed into the cab,
and struck up some sort of relationship with the
    driver.

That night,
on the bus coming home,
we were all a little embarrassed.
Especially me and the younglady in the green hat.
And we all started to say
in different ways
how hasty and foolish we had been.
But then, always having been a bitofalad,
i stood up and said it was a pity
that the world didnt nearly end every lunchtime,
and that we could always pretend.
And then it happened . . .

Quick asa crash
we all changed partners,
and soon the bus was aquiver
with white, mothball bodies doing naughty things.

And the next day
and everyday
In everybus
In everystreet
In everytown
In everycountry

People pretended
that the world was coming to an end at lunchtime.
It still hasnt
Although in a way it has.

ROGER MCGOUGH

Alone

Each lover has a theory of his own
About the difference between the ache
Of being with his love, and being alone:

Why what, when dreaming, is dear flesh and bone
That really stirs the senses, when awake,
Appears a simulacrum of his own.

Narcissus disbelieves in the unknown;
He cannot join his image in the lake
So long as he assumes he is alone.

The child, the waterfall, the fire, the stone,
Are always up to mischief, though, and take
The universe for granted as their own.

The elderly, like Proust, are always prone
To think of love as a subjective fake;
The more they love, the more they feel alone.

Whatever view we hold, it must be shown
Why every lover has a wish to make
Some other kind of otherness his own:
Perhaps, in fact, we never are alone.

W. H. AUDEN

Fidelity

Fidelity and love are two different things, like a flower
 and a gem.
And love, like a flower, will fade, will change into
 something else
or it would not be flowery.

O flowers they fade because they are moving swiftly; a
 little torrent of life
leaps up to the summit of the stem, gleams, turns over
 round the bend
of the parabola of curved flight,
sinks, and is gone, like a cornet curving into the invisible.

O flowers they are all the time travelling
like cornets, and they come into our ken
for a day, for two days, and withdraw, slowly vanish again.

And we, we must take them on the wing, and let them go.
Embalmed flowers are not flowers, immortelles are not
 flowers;
flowers are just a motion, a swift motion, a coloured
 gesture;
that is their loveliness. And that is love.

But a gem is different. It lasts so much longer than we do
so much much much longer
that it seems to last forever.
Yet we know it is flowing away

as flowers are, and we are, only slower.
The wonderful slow flowing of the sapphire!

All flows, and every flow is related to every other flow.
Flowers and sapphires and us, diversely streaming.
In the old days, when sapphires were breathed upon and
     brought forth
during the wild orgasms of chaos
time was much slower, when the rocks came forth.
It took aeons to make a sapphire, aeons for it to pass away.

And a flower it takes a summer.

And man and woman are like the earth, that brings forth
     flowers
in summer, and love, but underneath is rock.
Older than flowers, older than ferns, older than
     foraminiferae
older than plasm altogether is the soul of a man
     underneath.

And when, throughout all the wild orgasms of love
slowly a gem forms, in the ancient, once-more-molten
     rocks
of two human hearts, two ancient rocks, a man's heart
     and a woman's,

that is the crystal of peace, the slow hard jewel of trust,
the sapphire of fidelity.
The gem of mutual peace emerging from the wild chaos
   of love.

D. H. Lawrence

from *Don Juan*

A long, long kiss, a kiss of youth and love
    And beauty, all concentrating like rays
Into one focus, kindled from above;
    Such kisses as belong to early days,
Where heart and soul and sense in concert move,
    And the blood's lava, and the pulse a blaze,
Each kiss a heart-quake, for a kiss's strength,
I think, it must be reckoned by its length.

By length I mean duration; theirs endured
    Heaven knows how long; no doubt they never reckoned,
And if they had, they could not have secured
    The sum of their sensations to a second.
They had not spoken, but they felt allured,
    As if their souls and lips each other beckoned,
Which, being joined, like swarming bees they clung,
Their hearts the flowers from whence the honey sprung.

Haidée spoke not of scruples, asked no vows
    Nor offered any; she had never heard
Of plight and promises to be a spouse,
    Or perils by a loving maid incurred.
She was all which pure ignorance allows
    And flew to her young mate like a young bird,
And never having dreamt of falsehood, she
Had not one word to say of constancy.

She loved and was belovèd, she adored
    And she was worshipped after nature's fashion.
Their intense souls, into each other poured,
    If souls could die, had perished in that passion,
But by degrees their senses were restored,
    Again to be o'ercome, again to dash on.
And beating 'gainst *his* bosom, Haidée's heart
Felt as if never more to beat apart.

LORD BYRON

Never Love Unless You Can

Never love unless you can
Bear with all the faults of man:
Men sometimes will jealous be,
Though but little cause they see;
And hang the head, as discontent,
And speak what straight they will repent.

Men that but one saint adore,
Make a show of love to more:
Beauty must be scorned in none,
Though but truly served in one:
For what is courtship, but disguise?
True hearts may have dissembling eyes.

Men, when their affairs require,
Must a while themselves retire,
Sometimes hunt, and sometimes hawk,
And not ever sit and talk.
If these and such like you can bear,
Then like, and love, and never fear!

THOMAS CAMPION

The Cinnamon Peeler

If I were a cinnamon peeler
I would ride your bed
and leave the yellow bark dust
on your pillow.

Your breasts and shoulders would reek
you could never walk through markets
without the profession of my fingers
floating over you. The blind would
stumble certain of whom they approached
though you might bathe
under rain gutters, monsoon.

Here on the upper thigh
at this smooth pasture
neighbour to your hair
or the crease
that cuts your back. This ankle.
You will be known among strangers
as the cinnamon peeler's wife.

I could hardly glance at you
before marriage
never touch you
– your keen nosed mother, your rough brothers.
I buried my hands

in saffron, disguised them
over smoking tar,
helped the honey gatherers . . .

When we swam once
I touched you in water
and our bodies remained free,
you could hold me and be blind of smell.
You climbed the bank and said

this is how you touch other women
the grass cutter's wife, the lime burner's daughter.
And you searched your arms
for the missing perfume

and knew

what good is it
to be the lime burner's daughter
left with no trace
as if not spoken to in the act of love
as if wounded without the pleasure of a scar.

You touched
your belly to my hands
in the dry air and said
I am the cinnamon
peeler's wife. Smell me.

MICHAEL ONDAATJE

Elegy 5

In summer's heat and mid-time of the day
To rest my limbs upon a bed I lay,
One window shut, the other open stood,
Which gave such light, as twinkles in a wood,
Like twilight glimpse at setting of the sun,
Or night being past, and yet not day begun.
Such light to shamefast maidens must be shown,
Where they must sport, and seem to be unknown.
Then came Corinna in a long loose gown,
Her white neck hid with tresses hanging down:
Resembling fair Semiramis going to bed
Or Layis of a thousand wooers sped.
I snatched her gown, being thin, the harm was small,
Yet strived she to be covered therewithal.
And striving thus as one that would be cast,
Betrayed herself, and yielded at the last.
Stark naked as she stood before mine eye,
Not one wen in her body could I spy.
What arms and shoulders did I touch and see,
How apt her breasts were to be pressed by me.
How smooth a belly under her waist saw I?
How large a leg, and what a lusty thigh?
To leave the rest, all liked me passing well,

I clinged her naked body, down she fell,
Judge you the rest, being tired she bade me kiss,
Jove send me more such afternoons as this.

OVID
Translated by Christopher Marlowe

From His Coy Mistress

*My early work is the fear of falling. Later on it became the
art of falling. Falling without hurting yourself. Later on it
is the art of hanging in there.*

Louise Bourgeois

Some days I think I will become a nun,
Book in a convent miles away,
Cut off my hair, and dress in black
Wanting to purge myself of men.

I'd kneel and pray and chant a lot,
Lie in a narrow bed, devising titles
Of unwritten books: *A Semiotics of Flirtation.*
Love? Some Concepts of the Verb 'To Sin'.

One thing's for sure, by wanting you
I'm not the woman that I think I am.
I cannot eat or sleep at all,
Just think about your lovely mouth,

The eerie moonlight and the Northern seas
And hope my body's still the temple
That you'd come upon, as if by chance,
To excavate a hundred years from now,

Burn incense in and dance and sing,
Oh yes, and weeping, worship in.

DERYN REES-JONES

Things Forbidden

The man that hath a handsome wife
   And keeps her as a treasure,
It is my chiefest joy of life
   To have her to my pleasure.

But if that man regardless were
   As though he cared not for her,
Though she were like to Venus fair,
   In faith I would abhor her.

If to do good I were restrained,
   And to do evil bidden,
I would be Puritan, I swear,
   For I love the thing forbidden.

It is the care that makes the theft;
   None loves the thing forsaken;
The bold and willing whore is left
   When the modest wench is taken.

She dull is that's too forwards bent;
   Not good, but want, is reason.
Fish at a feast, and flesh in Lent,
   Are never out of season.

ANON.

Hymn to Aphrodite

Aphrodite, bringer of confusion
to all the cities of the broad earth, approach
this capital fortified against Spring, and hear
the prayers of the millions

wearing their lives thin on concrete,
frayed by self-willed deadlines,
by giving and taking orders continually
(which is the worse?),

bowed by those engines of remote
control, the telephone, the computer
terminal, so emaciated by
the wrong sort of passions,

walking too fast round corners,
up stairs, along corridors, and back,
utterly bored in several rooms,
eating the Minutes,

Goddess, approach on the wings
of prolific sparrows, greedy pigeons,
forsake your Mediterranean shores,
turn to the North,

you who savage human possessions,
who promote the transfer of property
without will, cause those men who
turn beggars' crutches

into newspapers, the hard men who measure
the earth's crust in terms of profit-margins,
to lose their heads, briefly, to small-town
out-of-work nurses,

smile and melt those tight-clenched faces,
weave your wiles, beguile
the self-made men to flambée
steaks with an oil share,

shuffle – for you delight in this – the pairs,
you singular democrat, and join
rank unequals under your exacting yoke,
every rush-hour

let two who did not know each other
at breakfast get off the Tube at a station
neither needs, inhaling electricity,
belonging together,

and, just once in a while, lend
your magic girdle to a suffering wife
and reclaim her puzzled, wandering husband,
however briefly.

Aphrodite, deathless, throned in gold
above the capital's highest building, look down,
bewitch all human traffic, let jams over-
whelm the police force,

let girls saunter slow across wide boulevards
on the green light, their ineffable legs, oiled at the joints,
stirring a dark, treacherous philtre, let men
walking towards them

be confused to find they suddenly have
three legs, and let men behind just
shorten their stride and imagine a face
more beautiful than yours.

MICHAEL LEVENE

The Balcony

Mother of memories, mistress of mistresses,
All fond desires, all my sweetest tasks!
You give back the nights of lingering caresses,
Hearth-sweetness, the summer night's velvet mask –
Mother of memories, mistress of mistresses.

The evenings shot with a charcoal glow,
Balcony music, heady with rose;
How I drowned in the swell of your warm heart's flow!
We have often spoken what time can't foreclose –
The evenings shot with a charcoal glow.

The stars blink their greetings of ancient light;
How rich these evenings we take at the flood!
Leaning towards you, my queen of the night,
I thought I caught the very scent of your blood –
The stars blink their greetings of ancient light.

The night grew thick and heavy like a shroud,
And my eyes scarcely fathomed your pupils' charms
I gulped in your breath's sweetly poisonous cloud,
And your feet lay numb in my drowsy arms –
The night grew thick and heavy like a shroud.

I can summon at will all my happiest hours,
And relive my past buried in your lap;

Why should I crave such alien flowers
When I feed on your body's inexhaustible sap?
I can summon at will all my happiest hours.

These murmurs, these perfumes, these endless caresses!
Will they rise from a gulf unplumbed by our gaze,
As the reborn sun is haloed with tresses?
Are they bathed in the sea's phosphorescent glaze?
These murmurs, these perfumes, these endless caresses!

CHARLES BAUDELAIRE
Translated by Peter Forbes

Stargazing

The night is fine and dry. It falls and spreads
the cold sky with a million opposites
that, for a spell, seem like a million souls
and soon, none, and then, for what seems a long time,
one. Then of course it spins. What is better to do
than string out over the infinite dead spaces
the ancient beasts and spearmen of the human
mind, and if not the real ones, new ones?

But, try making them clear to one you love,
(whoever is standing by you is one you love
when pinioned by the stars): you will find it quite
impossible, but like her more for thinking
she sees that constellation.
After the wave of pain, you will turn to her
and, in an instant, change the universe
to a sky you were glad you came outside to see.

This is the act of all the descended gods
of every age and creed: to weary of all
that never ends, to take a human hand
and go back into the house.

GLYN MAXWELL

Delight in Disorder

A sweet disorder in the dress
Kindles in clothes a wantonness:
A lawn about the shoulders thrown
Into a fine distraction;
An erring lace, which here and there
Enthrals the crimson stomacher;
A cuff neglectful, and thereby
Ribbands to flow confusèdly;
A winning wave (deserving note)
In the tempestuous petticoat;
A careless shoestring, in whose tie
I see a wild civility:
Do more bewitch me, than when art
Is too precise in every part.

ROBERT HERRICK

Over and Elm and I

Nothing to recommend your feet
except that when you put them down
on Market Hill or Benet Street
you make a better town

Nothing to recommend your stance
except that anywhere you stand
soaks up your presence to enhance
all the surrounding land

No evidence you are a cure
but that the envelope you sealed
and hand-delivered to my door
held a St Neots field

Nothing but that you seem to reach
beyond the space you occupy
so that in March and Waterbeach
Over and Elm and Eye

pillows store imprints of your face
surprised to learn that there's a head
whose contact with a pillowcase
can so improve a bed

You hailed a taxi at the lights
now every single cab that turns
onto East Road like yours ignites
Even the downpour burns

In its stone pot the stand-up clock
turns to a flower on its stem
The county's little stations rock
I feel like one of them

SOPHIE HANNAH

from *The Perfect Stranger*

I was in digs now, locked away, but the other lodgers had
streams of visitors up and down the stairs past my door.
None of these disturbed me except one girl who went
'Pom pom POM' as she ran up to the room above. It was a
sound of extraordinary sweetness, musical, soft,
unselfconscious and happy. I began to listen out for it,
jump up from my table, throw open the door to catch a
glimpse of her as she passed, but I was always too late.
I asked the people upstairs who she was, described the
beautiful sound she made. They became rather guarded
and exchanged glances and hesitatingly admitted it just
might be Sally. I gathered she was someone special, not to
be discussed in the ordinary way, and became vaguely
curious to meet her . . .

One day I came face to face with a girl on the landing. It
was certainly her, whoever made that noise had to look as
she did. We stood and stared at each other too long for
comfort. I broke the moment and, excusing myself,
moved past her because it was too like the movies, or so I
thought to myself of that long, silent stare, and laughed.
She was tall and proud-looking with a slight round-
shouldered stoop that made me breathless, I didn't know
why.
   It is difficult to describe someone who is surrounded by
a special nimbus, perceived at once. But as this girl had
the same effect, in one way or another, on many others, I
must try. She had soft yellow hair, greeny-blue eyes, lovely

eyebrows below a broad, quiet forehead and the most perfect mouth I have ever seen; underneath her skin there were golden lights. I am not a good physiognomist, I find it distorts a face to see it in detail, and I imagine the peculiar, extraordinary charm of her face lay in its proportions and in its expression. When I first saw the friezes in the museum on the Acropolis I couldn't believe it, most of the girls are portraits of her. Her face, and above all her expression, belonged to the same ideal, golden time. But beautiful girls are, in a sense, two a penny. There was something even more arresting, something unique in her face. She had the simplicity of a young girl (she was nineteen) who found life good; but it was a simplicity that had somehow been earned, was, as it were, on the second time round. This second simplicity has the directness and potency of a natural force. She had the kind of beauty that can change but not diminish – it depended for so much of its power on the kind of person she was that it could only end when she did. One trembled for her (it was too good to survive) and was humbled at the same time, by a face that was more strongly alive than anyone else's, which contained an indestructible, fearless happiness. She shone.

A few days later we met at a small party and I stood at her side. We didn't speak much. I told her of the noise she made as she passed my door. And often on the days that followed when I got back to my room I found the words 'Poop, poop poop' written on a piece of paper lying on my table – her phonetic spelling of the noise I hadn't been there to hear. One night we made part of a party that went to the theatre together. This entailed her staying the night out of her college and I found her a room in the house where I was living. After saying goodnight I went upstairs back to my desk, I had an essay to write. After a few lines I felt I had to be sure she had everything she needed and went downstairs. She had, and I went back to my work. Another few lines and I knew it was no use. I went down again and she seemed to be waiting for me, her face luminous and amused. I did what I should have done days before, I took her in my arms and kissed her; every experience, however simple, has its maximum brilliance. This happens only once, and is so startlingly different from anything less than itself that it seems to contain indications of a strength and a joy far beyond it, a hint that we live only on the edges of a possibility.

P. J. KAVANAGH

Tests, Trials and Torments

Scarborough Fair

Can you make me a cambric shirt,
 Parsley, sage, rosemary, and thyme,
Without any seam or needlework?
 And you shall be a true lover of mine.

Can you wash it in yonder well,
 Parsley, sage, rosemary, and thyme,
Where never sprung water, nor rain ever fell?
 And you shall be a true lover of mine.

Can you dry it on yonder thorn,
 Parsley, sage, rosemary, and thyme,
Which never bore blossom since Adam was born?
 And you shall be a true lover of mine.

Now you've asked me questions three,
 Parsley, sage, rosemary, and thyme,
I hope you'll answer as many for me,
 And you shall be a true lover of mine.

Can you find me an acre of land,
 Parsley, sage, rosemary, and thyme,
Between the salt water and the sea sand?
 And you shall be a true lover of mine.

Can you plough it with a ram's horn,
 Parsley, sage, rosemary, and thyme,

And sow it all over with one pepper-corn?
    And you shall be a true lover of mine.

Can you reap it with a sickle of leather,
    Parsley, sage, rosemary, and thyme,
And bind it up with a peacock's feather?
    And you shall be a true lover of mine.

When you have done and finished your work,
    Parsley, sage, rosemary, and thyme,
Then come to me for your cambric shirt,
    And you shall be a true lover of mine.

ANON.

The Did-You-Come-Yets
of the Western World

When he says to you:
You look so beautiful
you smell so nice –
how I've missed you –
and did you come yet?

It means nothing,
and he is smaller
than a mouse's fart.

Don't listen to him . . .
Go to Annaghdown Pier
with your father's rod.
Don't necessarily hold out
for the biggest one;
oftentimes the biggest ones
are the smallest in the end.

Bring them all home,
but not together.
One by one is the trick;
avoid red herrings and scandal.

Maybe you could take two
on the shortest day of the year.
Time is the cheater here

not you, so don't worry.
Many will bite the usual bait;
they will talk their slippery way
through fine clothes and expensive perfume,
fishing up your independence.

These are
the did-you-come-yets of the western world,
the feather and fin rufflers.
Pity for them they have no wisdom.

Others will bite at any bait.
Maggot, suspender, or dead worm.
Throw them to the sharks.

In time one will crawl
out from under thigh-land.
Although drowning he will say,

'Woman I am terrified, why is this house shaking?'

And you'll know he's the one.

RITA ANN HIGGINS

Marriage

Should I get married? Should I be good?
Astound the girl next door with my velvet suit and faustus
     hood?
Don't take her to movies but to cemeteries
tell all about werewolf bathtubs and forked clarinets
then desire her and kiss her and all the preliminaries
and she going just so far and I understanding why
not getting angry saying You must feel! It's beautiful to
     feel!
Instead take her in my arms lean against an old crooked
     tombstone
and woo her the entire night the constellations in the sky –

When she introduces me to her parents
back straightened, hair finally combed, strangled by a tie,
should I sit knees together on their 3rd degree sofa
and not ask Where's the bathroom?
How else to feel other than I am,
often thinking Flash Gordon soap –
O how terrible it must be for a young man
seated before a family and the family thinking
We never saw him before! He wants our Mary Lou!
After tea and homemade cookies they ask What do you do
     for a living?

Should I tell them? Would they like me then?
Say All right get married, we're losing a daughter
but we're gaining a son –

And should I then ask Where's the bathroom?

O God, and the wedding! All her family and her friends
and only a handful of mine all scroungy and bearded
just wait to get at the drinks and food –
And the priest! he looking at me as if I masturbated
asking me Do you take this woman for your lawful
    wedded wife?
And I trembling what to say say Pie Glue!
I kiss the bride all those corny men slapping me on the
    back

She's all yours, boy! Ha-ha-ha!
And in their eyes you could see some obscene honeymoon
    going on –
Then all that absurd rice and clanky cans and shoes
Niagara Falls! Hordes of us! Husbands! Wives! Flowers!
    Chocolates!

All streaming into cozy hotels
All going to do the same thing tonight
The indifferent clerk he knowing what was going to
    happen
The lobby zombies they knowing what
The whistling elevator man he knowing
The winking bellboy knowing
Everybody knowing! I'd be almost inclined not to do
    anything!
Stay up all night! Stare that hotel clerk in the eye!
Screaming: I deny honeymoon! I deny honeymoon!
running rampant into those almost climactic suites
yelling Radio belly! Cat shovel!

O I'd live in Niagara forever! in a dark cave beneath the
    Falls
I'd sit there the Mad Honeymooner
devising ways to break marriages, a scourge of bigamy
a saint of divorce –

But I should get married I should be good
How nice it'd be to come home to her
and sit by the fireplace and she in the kitchen
aproned young and lovely wanting my baby
and so happy about me she burns the roast beef
and comes crying to me and I get up from my big papa
    chair
saying Christmas teeth! Radiant brains! Apple deaf!
God what a husband I'd make! Yes, I should get married!
So much to do! like sneaking into Mr Jones' house late at
    night
and cover his golf clubs with 1920 Norwegian books
Like hanging a picture of Rimbaud on the lawnmower
like pasting Tannu Tuva postage stamps all over the picket
    fence
like when Mrs Kindhead comes to collect for the
    Community Chest
grab her and tell her There are unfavourable omens in
    the sky!
And when the mayor comes to get my vote tell him
When are you going to stop people killing whales!
And when the milkman comes leave him a note in the
    bottle
Penguin dust, bring me penguin dust, I want penguin
    dust –

Yet if I should get married and it's Connecticut and snow
and she gives birth to a child and I am sleepless, worn,
up for nights, head bowed against a quiet window, the past
    behind me,
finding myself in the most common of situations a
    trembling man
knowledged with responsibility not twig-smear nor
    Roman coin soup –
O what would that be like!
Surely I'd give it for a nipple a rubber Tacitus
For a rattle a bag of broken Bach records
Tack Della Francesca all over its crib
Sew the Greek alphabet on its bib
And build for its playpen a roofless Parthenon

No, I doubt I'd be that kind of father
not rural not snow no quiet window
but hot smelly tight New York City
seven flights up roaches and rats in the walls
a fat Reichian wife screeching over potatoes Get a job!
And five nose running brats in love with Batman
And the neighbors all toothless and dry haired
like those hag masses of the 18th century
all wanting to come in and watch TV
The landlord wants his rent
Grocery store Blue Cross Gas & Electric Knights of
    Columbus
Impossible to lie back and dream Telephone snow, ghost
    parking –
No! I should not get married I should never get married!
But – imagine if I were married to a beautiful
    sophisticated woman

tall and pale wearing an elegant black dress and long black
    gloves
holding a cigarette holder in one hand and a highball in
    the other
and we lived high up in a penthouse with a huge window
from which we could see all of New York and ever farther
    on clearer days
No, can't imagine myself married to that pleasant prison
    dream –

O but what about love? I forget love
not that I am incapable of love
it's just that I see love as odd as wearing shoes –
I never wanted to marry a girl who was like my mother
And Ingrid Bergman was always impossible
And there's maybe a girl now but she's already married
And I don't like men and –
but there's got to be somebody!
Because what if I'm 60 years old and not married,
all alone in a furnished room with pee stains on my
    underwear
and everybody else is married! All the universe married
    but me!

Ah, yet well I know that were a woman possible as I am
    possible
then marriage would be possible –
Like SHE in her lonely alien gaud waiting her Egyptian
    lover
so I wait – bereft of 2,000 years and the bath of life.

GREGORY CORSO

The Faithful Wife

I am away from home
A hundred miles from the blue curtains
I made at Christmas and the table
My grandfather brought back from Sorrento.
I am a career woman at a conference.
I love my husband. I value
Both what I own and what I do.

I left the forsythias half yellow,
The bluebells – lifted from a wood in Suffolk
Last year – still tight, the mint surfacing.
I must sweep the paths when I get back.

And here for the past week you and I
Have been conducting a non-affair
That could not even be called flirtation
That could not be called anything
Except unusually straightforward desire,
Adultery in the heart.
Life is so short.

The programme is ending.
11.30 – Conference disperses.
I watch everybody leaving.
It feels like grief, like the guillotine.

Your turn now; go home
With the 'Good-bye, love'

You use to every personable woman.
Get in your large car which ten years ago
Was full of sand and children's things
On summer evenings.
You are middle-aged now, as I am.
Write your notes up,
Fix the rattling window,
Keep your marriage vows. As I shall.

PATRICIA BEER

For My Lover, Returning to His Wife

She is all there.
She was melted carefully down for you
and cast up from your childhood,
cast up from your one hundred favorite aggies.

She has always been there, my darling.
She is, in fact, exquisite.
Fireworks in the dull middle of February
and as real as a cast-iron pot.

Let's face it, I have been momentary.
A luxury. A bright red sloop in the harbor.
My hair rising like smoke from the car window.
Littleneck clams out of season.
She is more than that. She is your have to have,
has grown you your practical your tropical growth.
This is not an experiment. She is all harmony.
She sees to oars and oarlocks for the dinghy,

has placed wild flowers at the window at breakfast,
sat by the potter's wheel at midday,
set forth three children under the moon,
three cherubs drawn by Michelangelo,

done this with her legs spread out
in the terrible months in the chapel.
If you glance up, the children are there
like delicate balloons resting on the ceiling.

Oh, how can, how can you ask me again,
It only brings me sorrow.
The same thing I want from you today,
I would want again tomorrow.

I got a letter on a lonesome day,
It was from her ship a-sailin',
Saying I don't know when I'll be comin' back again,
It depends on how I'm a-feelin'.

Well, if you, my love, must think that-a-way,
I'm sure your mind is roamin'.
I'm sure your heart is not with me,
But with the country to where you're goin'.

So take heed, take heed of the western wind,
Take heed of the stormy weather.
And yes, there's something you can send back to me,
Spanish boots of Spanish leather.

BOB DYLAN

Two in the Campagna

I

I wonder do you feel today
 As I have felt since, hand in hand,
We sat down on the grass, to stray
 In spirit better through the land,
This morn of Rome and May?

II

For me, I touched a thought, I know,
 Has tantalized me many times,
(Like turns of thread the spiders throw
 Mocking across our path) for rhymes
To catch at and let go.

III

Help me to hold it! First it left
 The yellowing fennel, run to seed
There, branching from the brickwork's cleft,
 Some old tomb's ruin: yonder weed
Took up the floating weft,

IV

Where one small orange cup amassed
    Five beetles, – blind and green they grope
Among the honey-meal: and last,
    Everywhere on the grassy slope
I traced it. Hold it fast!

V

The champaign with its endless fleece
    Of feathery grasses everywhere!
Silence and passion, joy and peace,
    An everlasting wash of air –
Rome's ghost since her decease.

VI

Such life here, through such lengths of hours,
    Such miracles performed in play,
Such primal naked forms of flowers,
    Such letting nature have her way
While heaven looks from its towers!

VII

How say you? Let us, O my dove,
    Let us be unashamed of soul,
As earth lies bare to heaven above!
    How is it under our control
To love or not to love?

VIII

I would that you were all to me,
     You that are just so much, no more.
Nor yours nor mine, nor slave nor free!
     Where does the fault lie? What the core
O' the wound, since wound must be?

IX

I would I could adopt your will,
     See with your eyes, and set my heart
Beating by yours, and drink my fill
     At your soul's springs, – your part my part
In life, for good and ill.

X

No. I yearn upward, touch you close,
     Then stand away. I kiss your cheek,
Catch your soul's warmth, – I pluck the rose
     And love it more than tongue can speak –
Then the good minute goes.

XI

Already how am I so far
     Out of that minute? Must I go
Still like the thistle-ball, no bar,
     Onward, whenever light winds blow,
Fixed by no friendly star?

XII

Just when I seemed about to learn!
    Where is the thread now? Off again!
The old trick! Only I discern –
    Infinite passion, and the pain
Of finite hearts that yearn.

ROBERT BROWNING

from Fifty Sonnets

IX

I don't know what you want from me. We talk
about a lot of things, but never that.
And if I asked, I'd break the tacit rules
of this as-modern-as-they-come affair –
this marvellous, no-strings, no-rules affair;
this minefield of exact, unwritten rules
surrounded by barbed wire of silence. That
is something of a pity, since we talk
about a lot of things, but I don't know –
and maybe never will, since if I asked
I'd break the tacit rules – quite what you want
from me – and minefields (modern ones) with no
strings (just barbed wire) we cross with care, unasked
questions buried, like so much else we want.

ELEANOR BROWN

She Moved through the Fair

My young love said to me, 'My brothers won't mind,
And my parents won't slight you for your lack of kind.'
Then she stepped away from me, and this she did say,
'It will not be long, love, till our wedding day.'

She stepped away from me and she moved through the
   fair,
And fondly I watched her go here and go there,
Then she went her way homeward with one star awake,
As the swan in the evening moves over the lake.

The people were saying no two were e'er wed
But one had a sorrow that never was said,
And I smiled as she passed with her goods and her gear,
And that was the last that I saw of my dear.

I dreamt it last night that my young love came in,
So softly she entered, her feet made no din;
She came close beside me, and this she did say,
'It will not be long, love, till our wedding day.'

PADRAIC COLUM

Westron Wynde

Westron wynde when will thou blow
The small rain down can rain –
Christ if my love were in my arms
And I in my bed again!

ANON.

Delay

The radiance of that star that leans on me
Was shining years ago. The light that now
Glitters up there my eye may never see,
And so the time lag teases me with how

Love that loves now may not reach me until
Its first desire is spent. The star's impulse
Must wait for eyes to claim it beautiful
And love arrived may find us somewhere else.

ELIZABETH JENNINGS

Faintheart in a Railway Train

At nine in the morning there passed a church,
At ten there passed me by the sea,
At twelve a town of smoke and smirch,
At two a forest of oak and birch,
    And then, on a platform, she:

A radiant stranger, who saw not me.
I said, 'Get out to her do I dare?'
But I kept my seat in my search for a plea,
And the wheels moved on. O could it but be
    That I had alighted there!

THOMAS HARDY

from *Amours de Voyage*

VI CLAUDE TO EUSTACE

Juxtaposition, in fine; and what is juxtaposition?
Look you, we travel along in the railway-carriage, or
steamer,
And, *pour passer le temps*, till the tedious journey be ended,
Lay aside paper or book, to talk with the girl that is next
one;
And, *pour passer le temps*, with the terminus all but in
prospect,
Talk of eternal ties and marriages made in heaven.
    Ah, did we really accept with a perfect heart the
    illusion!
Ah, did we really believe that the Present indeed is the
Only!
Or through all transmutation, all shock and convulsion of
passion,
Feel we could carry undimmed, unextinguished, the light
of our knowledge!
    But for his funeral train which the bridegroom
    sees in the distance,
Would he so joyfully, think you, fall in with the marriage-
procession?
But for that final discharge, would he dare to enlist in
that service?
But for that certain release, ever sign to that perilous
contract?

But for that exit secure, ever bend to that treacherous
doorway? –
Ah, but the bride, meantime, – do you think she sees it as
he does?
But for the steady fore-sense of a freer and larger
existence,
Think you that man could consent to be circumscribed
here into action?
But for assurance within of a limitless ocean divine, o'er
Whose great tranquil depths unconscious the wind-tost
surface
Breaks into ripples of trouble that come and change and
endure not, –
But that in this, of a truth, we have our being, and know
it,
Think you we men could submit to live and move as we
do here?
Ah, but the women, – God bless them! they don't think at
all about it.
Yet we must eat and drink, as you say. And as
limited beings
Scarcely can hope to attain upon earth to an Actual
Abstract,
Leaving to God contemplation, to His hands knowledge
confiding,
Sure that in us if it perish, in Him it abideth and dies not,
Let us in His sight accomplish our petty particular
doings, –
Yes, and contented sit down to the victual that He has
provided.
Allah is great, no doubt, and Juxtaposition his prophet.
Ah, but the women, alas! they don't look at it in that way.

Juxtaposition is great; – but, my friend, I fear me,
the maiden
Hardly would thank or acknowledge the lover that sought
to obtain her,
Not as the thing he would wish, but the thing he must
even put up with, –
Hardly would tender her hand to the wooer that candidly
told her
That she is but for a space, an *ad-interim* solace and
pleasure, –
That in the end she shall yield to a perfect and absolute
something,
Which I then for myself shall behold, and not another, –
Which, amid fondest endearments, meantime I forget not,
forsake not.
Ah, ye feminine souls, so loving and so exacting,
Since we cannot escape, must we even submit to deceive
you?
Since so cruel is truth, sincerity shocks and revolts you,
Will you have us your slaves to lie to you, flatter and –
leave you?

ARTHUR HUGH CLOUGH

Sonnet xxx

Love is not all: it is not meat nor drink
Nor slumber nor a roof against the rain;
Nor yet a floating spar to men that sink
And rise and sink and rise and sink again;
Love can not fill the thickened lung with breath,
Nor clean the blood, nor set the fractured bone;
Yet many a man is making friends with death
Even as I speak, for lack of love alone.
It well may be that in a difficult hour,
Pinned down by pain and moaning for release,
Or nagged by want past resolution's power,
I might be driven to sell your love for peace,
Or trade the memory of this night for food.
It well may be. I do not think I would.

EDNA ST VINCENT MILLAY

'Think'st thou to seduce me then with words that have no meaning?'

Think'st thou to seduce me then with words that have no
    meaning?
Parrots so can learn to prate, our speech by pieces
    gleaning:
Nurses teach their children so about the time of weaning.

Learn to speak first, then to woo: to wooing, much
    pertaineth:
He that courts us wanting art, soon falters when he
    feigneth,
Looks asquint on his discourse, and smiles, when he
    complaineth.

Skilful anglers hide their hooks, fit baits for every season;
But with crooked pins fish thou, as babes do, that want
    reason:
Gudgeons only can be caught with such poor tricks of
    treason.

Ruth forgive me, if I erred from human heart's
   compassion,
When I laughed sometimes too much to see thy foolish
   fashion:
But, alas, who less could do that found so good occasion!

THOMAS CAMPION

'Never seek to tell thy love'

Never seek to tell thy love,
Love that never told can be;
For the gentle wind does move
Silently, invisibly.

I told my love, I told my love.
I told her all my heart;
Trembling, cold, in ghastly fears,
Ah! she doth depart.

Soon as she was gone from me,
A traveller came by,
Silently, invisibly:
He took her with a sigh.

WILLIAM BLAKE

'When love its utmost vigour does employ'

When love its utmost vigour does employ,
Even then, 'tis but a restless wandering joy:
Nor knows the lover, in that wild excess,
With hands or eyes, what first he would possess:
But strains at all; and fastening where he strains,
Too closely presses with his frantic pains:
With biting kisses hurts the twining fair,
Which shews his joys imperfect, unsincere:
For stung with inward rage, he flings around,
And strives to avenge the smart on that which gave the
    wound.
But love those eager bitings does restrain,
And mingling pleasure mollifies the pain.
For ardent hope still flatters anxious grief,
And sends him to his foe to seek relief:
Which yet the nature of the thing denies;
For love, and love alone of all our joys
By full possession does but fan the fire,
The more we still enjoy, the more we still desire.
Nature for meat, and drink provides a space;
And when received they fill their certain place;
Hence thirst and hunger may be satisfied,
But this repletion is to love denied:
Form, feature, colour, whatsoe're delight
Provokes the lovers' endless appetite,
These fill no space, nor can we thence remove
With lips, or hands, or all our instruments of love:
In our deluded grasp we nothing find,

But thin aerial shapes, that fleet before the mind.
As he who in a dream with drought is cursed
And finds no real drink to quench his thirst,
Runs to imagined lakes his heat to steep,
And vainly swills and labours in his sleep;
So love with phantoms cheats our longing eyes,
Which hourly seeing never satisfies;
Our hands pull nothing from the parts they strain,
But wander over the lovely limbs in vain:
Nor when the youthful pair more closely join,
When hands in hands they lock, and thighs in thighs they
   twine
Just in the raging foam of full desire,
When both press on, both murmur, both expire,
They grip, they squeeze, their humid tongues they dart,
As each would force their way to the other's heart:
In vain; they only cruise about the coast,
For bodies cannot pierce, nor be in bodies lost:
As sure they strive to be, when both engage,
In that tumultuous momentary rage;
So tangled in the nets of love they lie,
Till man dissolves in that excess of joy.
Then, when the gathered bag has burst its way,
And ebbing tides the slackened nerves betray,
A pause ensues; and nature nods a while,
Till with recruited rage new spirits boil;
And then the same vain violence returns,
With flames renewed the erected furnace burns.
Again they in each other would be lost,

But still by adamantine bars are crossed;
All ways they try, successless all they prove,
To cure the secret sore of lingering love.

LUCRETIUS
Translated by John Dryden

The Looking-Glass

Getting a man to love you is easy
Only be honest about your wants as
Woman. Stand nude before the glass with him
So that he sees himself the stronger one
And believes it so, and you so much more
Softer, younger, lovelier . . . Admit your
Admiration. Notice the perfection
Of his limbs, his eyes reddening under
The shower, the shy walk across the bathroom floor,
Dropping towels, and the jerky way he
Urinates. All the fond details that make
Him male and your only man. Gift him all,
Gift him what makes you woman, the scent of
Long hair, the musk of sweat between the breasts,
The warm shock of menstrual blood, and all your
Endless female hungers. Oh yes, getting
A man to love is easy, but living
Without him afterwards may have to be
Faced. A living without life when you move
Around, meeting strangers, with your eyes that
Gave up their search, with ears that hear only
His last voice calling out your name and your
Body which once under his touch had gleamed
Like burnished brass, now drab and destitute.

KAMALA DAS

In Rainy September

In rainy September, when leaves grow down to the dark,
I put my forehead down to the damp, seaweed-smelling
    sand.
The time has come. I have put off choosing for years,
Perhaps whole lives. The fern has no choice but to live;
For this crime it receives earth, water, and night.

We close the door. 'I have no claim on you.'
Dusk comes. 'The love I have had with you is enough.'
We know we could live apart from one another.
The sheldrake floats apart from the flock.
The oaktree puts out leaves alone on the lonely hillside.

Men and women before us have accomplished this.
I would see you, and you me, once a year.
We would be two kernels, and not be planted.
We stay in the room, door closed, lights.
I weep with you without shame and without honor.

ROBERT BLY

The Bonny Boy

I once had a boy and a bonny, bonny boy
And thought to make him my own;
But he loves another much better than me
And has taken his flight and is gone
And has taken his flight and is gone

Since he is gone now let him go
No longer for him will I mourn;
If he loves another much better than me
Then I hope he will never return
Then I hope he will never return

I walked up the forest and down the green fields
Like one distracted in mind
I halloed and I whooped and I played upon my flute
But no bonny boy could I find
But no bonny boy could I find

I looked in the East, I looked in the West
The weather being hot and calm;
And there I did spy my bonny bonny boy
With another love close in his arms
With another love close in his arms

But I hasted by and never cast an eye
Though he thought I had been in love bound;
I loved him so well, no notice I took

But was glad when him I had found
But was glad when him I had found

He took me upon his dissembling knee
And looked me upright in my face;
He gave to me a dissembling kiss
But his heart was in another place
But his heart was in another place

Now you have got my bonny bonny boy
Be kind to my boy if you can;
For though he's none of mine he's a pleasure in my mind
And I'll walk with that boy now and then
And I'll walk with that boy now and then

ANON.

from *Don Juan*

Man's love is of his life a thing apart,
    'Tis woman's whole existence. Man may range
The court, camp, church, the vessel, and the mart;
    Sword, gown, gain, glory offer in exchange
Pride, fame, ambition to fill up his heart,
    And few there are whom these cannot estrange.
Man has all these resources, we but one,
To mourn alone the love which has undone.

LORD BYRON

XXIII

As an unperfect actor on the stage,
Who with his fear is put besides his part,
Or some fierce thing replete with too much rage,
Whose strength's abundance weakens his own heart;
So I, for fear of trust, forget to say
The perfect ceremony of love's rite,
And in mine own love's strength seem to decay,
O'ercharg'd with burthen of mine own love's might.
O let my books be then the eloquence
And dumb presagers of my speaking breast;
Who plead for love, and look for recompense,
More than that tongue that more hath more express'd.
   O learn to read what silent love hath writ:
   To hear with eyes belongs to love's fine wit.

LVII

Being your slave, what should I do but tend
Upon the hours and times of your desire?
I have no precious time at all to spend,
Nor services to do, till you require.
Nor dare I chide the world-without-end hour,
Whilst I, my sovereign, watch the clock for you,
Nor think the bitterness of absence sour,
When you have bid your servant once adieu;
Nor dare I question with my jealous thought

Where you may be, or your affairs suppose,
But, like a sad slave, stay and think of nought,
Save, where you are how happy you make those:
    So true a fool is love, that in your will
    (Though you do anything) he thinks no ill.

CVI

Let me not to the marriage of true minds
Admit impediments. Love is not love
Which alters when it alteration finds,
Or bends with the remover to remove:
O no; it is an ever-fixed mark,
That looks on tempests, and is never shaken;
It is the star to every wandering bark,
Whose worth's unknown, although his height be taken.
Love's not Time's fool, though rosy lips and cheeks
Within his bending sickle's compass come;
Love alters not with his brief hours and weeks,
But bears it out even to the edge of doom.
    If this be error, and upon me prov'd,
    I never writ, nor no man ever lov'd.

CXXX

My mistress' eyes are nothing like the sun;
Coral is far more red than her lips' red:
If snow be white, why then her breasts are dun;
If hairs be wires, black wires grow on her head.
I have seen roses damask'd, red and white,
But no such roses see I in her cheeks;
And in some perfumes is there more delight

Than in the breath that from my mistress reeks.
I love to hear her speak, – yet well I know
That music hath a far more pleasing sound;
I grant I never saw a goddess go, –
My mistress, when she walks, treads on the ground;
    And yet, by Heaven, I think my love as rare
    As any she belied with false compare.

CXXXVIII

When my love swears that she is made of truth,
I do believe her, though I know, she lies;
That she might think me some untutor'd youth,
Unlearned in the world's false subtilties.
Thus vainly thinking that, she thinks me young,
Although she knows my days are past the best,
Simply I credit her false-speaking tongue;
On both sides thus is simple truth supprest.
But wherefore says she not she is unjust?
And wherefore say not I that I am old?
O, love's best habit is in seeming trust,
And age in love loves not to have years told:
    Therefore I lie with her, and she with me,
    And in our faults by lies we flatter'd be.

CXLVII

My love is as a fever, longing still
For that which longer nurseth the disease;
Feeding on that which doth preserve the ill,
The uncertain sickly appetite to please.
My reason, the physician to my love,

Angry that his prescriptions are not kept,
Hath left me, and I desperate now approve
Desire is death, which physic did except.
Past cure I am, now reason is past care,
And frantic mad with evermore unrest;
My thought and my discourse as mad men's are,
At random from the truth vainly express'd;
    For I have sworn thee fair, and thought thee bright,
    Who art as black as hell, as dark as night.

CLI

Love is too young to know what conscience is;
Yet who knows not, conscience is born of love?
Then, gentle cheater, urge not my amiss,
Lest guilty of my faults thy sweet self prove.
For thou betraying me, I do betray
My nobler part to my gross body's treason;
My soul doth tell my body that he may
Triumph in love; flesh stays no farther reason;
But, rising as thy name, doth point out thee
As his triumphant prize. Proud of this pride,
He is contented thy poor drudge to be,
To stand in thy affairs, fall by thy side,
    No want of conscience hold it that I call
    Her – love, for whose dear love I rise and fall.

WILLIAM SHAKESPEARE

'Waiting for breakfast,
while she brushed her hair'

Waiting for breakfast, while she brushed her hair,
I looked down at the empty hotel yard
Once meant for coaches. Cobblestones were wet,
But sent no light back to the loaded sky,
Sunk as it was with mist down to the roofs.
Drainpipes and fire-escape climbed up
Past rooms still burning their electric light:
I thought: Featureless morning, featureless night.

Misjudgment: for the stones slept, and the mist
Wandered absolvingly past all it touched,
Yet hung like a stayed breath; the lights burnt on,
Pin-points of undisturbed excitement; beyond the glass
The colourless vial of day painlessly spilled
My world back after a year, my lost lost world
Like a cropping deer strayed near my path again,
Bewaring the mind's least clutch. Turning, I kissed her,
Easily for sheer joy tipping the balance to love.

But, tender visiting,
Fallow as a deer or an unforced field,
How would you have me? Towards your grace
My promises meet and lock and race like rivers,
But only when you choose. Are you jealous of her?

Will you refuse to come till I have sent
Her terribly away, importantly live
Part invalid, part baby, and part saint?

PHILIP LARKIN

A Renunciation

We, that did nothing study but the way
To love each other, with which thoughts the day
Rose with delight to us and with them set,
Must learn the hateful art, how to forget.
We, that did nothing wish that Heaven could give
Beyond ourselves, nor did desire to live
Beyond that wish, all these now cancel must,
As if not writ in faith, but words and dust.
Yet witness those clear vows which lovers make,
Witness the chaste desires that never break
Into unruly heats; witness that breast
Which in thy bosom anchored his whole rest –
'T is no default in us: I dare acquite
Thy maiden faith, thy purpose fair and white
As thy pure self. Cross planets did envy
Us to each other, and Heaven did untie
Faster than vows could bind. Oh that the stars,
When lovers meet, should stand opposed in wars!
Since, then, some higher destinies command,
Let us not strive, nor labour to withstand
What is past help. The longest date of grief
Can never yield a hope of our relief.
Fold back our arms; take home our fruitless loves,
That must new fortunes try, like turtle-doves
Dislodgèd from their haunts; we must in tears
Unwind a love knit up in many years.
In this last kiss I here surrender thee
Back to thyself – so thou again art free;

Thou in another, sad as that, resend
The truest heart that lover e'er did lend.
Now turn from each; so fare our severed hearts
As the divorced soul from her body parts.

HENRY KING

Farewell Nancy

O farewell me dearest Nancy for now I must leave you,
All across to the West Indies our course we must steer,
Don't let me long voyage to sorry and grieve you
For you know I'll be back in the springtime of the year.

She says, 'Like some little seaboy I'll dress and I'll go
   with you,
In the midst of all danger your help I'll remain;
In the cold stormy weather when the winds they are
   a-blowin',
O me love I'll be there to reel your top-sail.'

O your pretty little hands they can't manage our tackle,
Your delicate feet in our clogs they'll cut so;
Your little behind, love, would freeze in the wynde, love –
I would have you at home when the stormy winds do blow.

So farewell me lovely Nancy for now I must leave you,
All across the Western Ocean I am bound far away;
Although we have parted, me love be true hearted
For you know I'll be back in the springtime of the year.

ANON.

from Marburg

I quivered. I flared up, and then was extinguished.
I shook. I had made a proposal – but late,
Too late. I was scared, and she had refused me.
I pity her tears, am more blessed than a saint.

I stepped into the square. I could be counted
Among the twice-born. Every leaf on the lime,
Every brick was alive, caring nothing for me,
And reared up to take leave for the last time.

The paving-stones glowed and the street's brow was
   swarthy.
From under their lids the cobbles looked grim,
Scowled up at the sky, and the wind like a boatman
Was rowing through limes. And each was an emblem.

Be that as it may, I avoided their glances,
Averted my gaze from their greeting or scowling.
I wanted no news of their getting and spending.
I had to get out, so as not to start howling.

BORIS PASTERNAK
Translated by Jon Stallworthy and Peter France

'They flee from me that sometime did me seek'

They flee from me that sometime did me seek
   With naked foot stalking in my chamber.
I have seen them gentle, tame and meek
   That now are wild and do not remember
   That sometime they put themselves in danger
To take bread at my hand; and now they range
Busily seeking with a continual change.

Thanked be fortune, it hath been otherwise
   Twenty times better; but once in special,
In thin array after a pleasant guise,
   When her loose gown from her shoulders did fall,
   And she me caught in her arms long and small;
Therewith all sweetly did me kiss,
And softly said, *'Dear heart, how like you this?'*

It was no dream: I lay broad waking.
   But all is turned thorough my gentleness
Into a strange fashion of forsaking,
   And I have leave to go of her goodness,
   And she also to use newfangleness.
But since that I so kindly am served,
I would fain know what she hath deserved.

SIR THOMAS WYATT

The Beloved

I wrote this fine glossy poem
about how the true beloved is always ineffable,
the one at the palace window
when the purple light of storm astounds the forest,
the one whose touch is the breeze of April,
the one with breasts of pearl swaying urgent toward the
   mouth of dream,
cloud-sister of Grace Kelly,
always finally that one in azure kimono

and never the contingent one who flosses
and collides with you in the kitchen
and wants forever to lose five pounds
and notices the smell of your sneakers
and remembers guys with stronger arms.
I wrote the poem and felt kind of brave
and rather ineffable myself
and I kind of saw Apollo in the mirror

so then I published the poem in a smooth journal
dedicated to the Other World that words can make –
world, or only a superb hotel? –

so then my wife reads the poem
and she looks at me: her gray-green eyes
moving in those subtle motions that eyes make
when they're anxious to see something true.

Looking into her eyes then I feel
not like a bad husband really but like a guy
half an inch shorter than he thought
whose poem didn't have the guts to be complicated.

MARK HALLIDAY

The Water Is Wide

The water is wide, I can't swim o'er
Nor do I have wings to fly
Give me a boat that can carry two
And both shall row, my love and I

A ship there is and she sails the sea
She's loaded deep as deep can be
But not so deep as the love I'm in
I know not if I sink or swim

I leaned my back against an oak
Thinking it was a trusty tree
But first it swayed and then it broke
So did my love prove false to me

Oh love is handsome and love is kind
Sweet as flower when first it is new
But love grows old and waxes cold
And fades away like the morning dew

Must I go bound while you go free
Must I love a man who doesn't love me
Must I be born with so little art
As to love a man who'll break my heart

ANON.

'Sigh no more, ladies, sigh no more'

Sigh no more, ladies, sigh no more.
Men were deceivers ever,
One foot in sea, and one on shore;
To one thing constant never.
Then sigh not so,
But let them go,
And be you blithe and bonny,
Converting all your sounds of woe
Into Hey nonny, nonny.

Sing no more ditties, sing no moe,
Of dumps so dull and heavy!
The fraud of men was ever so,
Since summer first was leavy.
Then sigh not so,
But let them go,
And be you blithe and bonny,
Converting all your sounds of woe
Into Hey nonny, nonny.

WILLIAM SHAKESPEARE

A Woman's Heart

O faithless world, and thy most faithless part,
    A woman's heart!
The true shop of variety, where sits
    Nothing but fits
And fevers of desire, and pangs of love,
    Which toys remove.
Why was she born to please? or I to trust
    Words writ in dust,
Suffering her eyes to govern my despair,
    My pain for air;
And fruit of time rewarded with untruth,
    The food of youth?
Untrue she was; yet I believed her eyes,
    Instructed spies,
Till I was taught that love was but a school
    To breed a fool.

Or sought she more, by triumphs of denial,
    To make a trial
How far her smiles commanded my weakness?
    Yield and confess!
Excuse no more thy folly; but, for cure,
    Blush and endure

As well thy shame as passions that were vain;
And think, 't is gain,
To know that love lodged in a woman's breast
Is but a guest.

SIR HENRY WOTTON

'If all the world and love were young'

If all the world and love were young,
And truth in every shepherd's tongue,
These pretty pleasures might me move
To live with thee and be thy love.

Time drives the flocks from field to fold,
When rivers rage and rocks grow cold,
And Philomel becometh dumb;
The rest complain of cares to come.

The flowers do fade, and wanton fields
To wayward winter reckoning yields;
A honey tongue, a heart of gall,
Is fancy's spring, but sorrow's fall.

Thy gowns, thy shoes, thy beds of roses,
Thy cap, thy kirtle, and thy posies
Soon break, soon wither, soon forgotten,
In folly ripe, in reason rotten.

Thy belt of straw and ivy buds,
Thy coral clasps and amber studs,
All these in me no means can move
To come to thee and be thy love.

But could youth last and love still breed,
Had joys no date nor age no need,
Then these delights my mind might move
To live with thee and be thy love.

SIR WALTER RALEGH

Hawthorn

May stinks. Why do we like it so?
For its rust of buds, as last snow strikes at hills,
For freckled, opened white which spills
Down dull lanes, shines to clouded skies,
Because it is early summer. So
The season I married, ten years ago
I walked through a town I longed to leave
Down by the river; heard evening breathe,
The swallows swish low. Now, I thought
All things may happen, from this day:
I was right, oh and wrong, sweet stink of the may.

ALISON BRACKENBURY

Life Is Very Long

Life is very long. A few mistakes, a few
occasions of some wonder, a few wrongs.
Nothing remains of the day we said goodbye
to the harbour, and I kissed you
on the cheek and you stilled because
you thought someone might be looking.
We stood on the breakwater strand
and faced town and a small figure
came towards us waving his pale hands
and failed completely to take our picture.
You walked all the way back holding your hat
and the whole-earth shampoo bottle
and I promised you a hot bath
if we only could get home before absolute night fell.
And now I do not know if you still care
or how much and I hold discourse
with thin air while out there on the cove
your hat is still pulled and that kiss still burns.

ATAR HADARI

from *Ideas Mirrour*

SONNET LXI

Since there's no help, come let us kiss and part –
Nay, I have done: you get no more of me;
And I am glad, yea glad with all my heart,
That thus so cleanly I myself can free.
Shake hands for ever, cancel all our vows,
And when we meet at any time again,
Be it not seen in either of our brows
That we one jot of former love retain.
Now at the last gasp of love's latest breath,
When, his pulse failing, passion speechless lies,
When faith is kneeling by his bed of death,
And innocence is closing up his eyes,
   Now if thou wouldst, when all have given him over,
   From death to life thou mightst him yet recover.

MICHAEL DRAYTON

Imperial

Is it normal to get this wet? Baby, I'm frightened –
I covered her mouth with my own;
she lay in my arms till the storm-window brightened
and stood at our heads like a stone

After months of jaw jaw, determined that neither
win ground, or be handed the edge,
we gave ourselves up, one to the other
like prisoners over a bridge

and no trade was ever so fair or so tender;
so where was the flaw in the plan,
the night we lay down on the flag of surrender
and woke on the flag of Japan

DON PATERSON

Time Was Away

Meeting Point

Time was away and somewhere else,
There were two glasses and two chairs
And two people with the one pulse
(Somebody stopped the moving stairs):
Time was away and somewhere else.

And they were neither up nor down;
The stream's music did not stop
Flowing through heather, limpid brown,
Although they sat in a coffee shop
And they were neither up nor down.

The bell was silent in the air
Holding its inverted poise –
Between the clang and clang a flower,
A brazen calyx of no noise:
The bell was silent in the air.

The camels crossed the miles of sand
That stretched around the cups and plates;
The desert was their own, they planned
To portion out the stars and dates:
The camels crossed the miles of sand.

Time was away and somewhere else.
The waiter did not come, the clock

Forgot them and the radio waltz
Came out like water from a rock:
Time was away and somewhere else.

Her fingers flicked away the ash
That bloomed again in tropic trees:
Not caring if the markets crash
When they had forests such as these,
Her fingers flicked away the ash.

God or whatever means the Good
Be praised that time can stop like this,
That what the heart has understood
Can verify in the body's peace
God or whatever means the Good.

Time was away and she was here
And life no longer what it was,
The bell was silent in the air
And all the room one glow because
Time was away and she was here.

LOUIS MACNEICE

Now

Out of your whole life give but a moment!
All of your life that has gone before,
All to come after it, – so you ignore
So you make perfect the present, – condense,
In a rapture of rage, for perfection's endowment,
Thought and feeling and soul and sense –
Merged in a moment which gives me at last
You around me for once, you beneath me, above me –
Me – sure that despite of time future, time past, –
This tick of our life-time's one moment you love me!
How long such suspension may linger? Ah, Sweet –
The moment eternal – just that and no more –
When ecstasy's utmost we clutch at the core
While cheeks burn, arms open, eyes shut and lips meet!

ROBERT BROWNING

A Birthday

My heart is like a singing bird
   Whose nest is in a watered shoot:
My heart is like an apple-tree
   Whose boughs are bent with thickset fruit;
My heart is like a rainbow shell
   That paddles in a halcyon sea;
My heart is gladder than all these
   Because my love is come to me.

Raise me a dais of silk and down;
   Hang it with vair and purple dyes;
Carve it in doves and pomegranates,
   And peacocks with a hundred eyes;
Work it in gold and silver grapes,
   In leaves and silver fleur-de-lys;
Because the birthday of my life
   Is come, my love is come to me.

CHRISTINA ROSSETTI

In a Bath Teashop

'Let us not speak, for the love we bear one another –
    Let us hold hands and look.'
She, such a very ordinary little woman;
    He, such a thumping crook;
But both, for a moment, little lower than the angels
    In the teashop's ingle-nook.

JOHN BETJEMAN

Collusion

Your face, flickering through green glass.
Wine tonight: a bottle's deft appeal.
(Another holds a candle.) Happiness –
Sloping-shouldered, with a touch of guile

To see you through. Inconstant, shifting face,
You stir the memory: french fries, the time
We tried the couch, our waltz – such common taste.
Happy days, my love – and more to come.

Obsessive, your yen for fixing things.
I watch for the next move: that sway across
The room, tug at a zip, those flutterings
Of shadow on the curtain – like vast moths . . .

Love, the old dance. Our gaudy night.
We drift unconscious, in deceptive light.

HUMPHREY CLUCAS

After Paradise

Don't run anymore. Quiet. How softly it rains
On the roofs of the city. How perfect
All things are. Now, for the two of you
Waking up in a royal bed by a garret window.
For a man and a woman. For one plant divided
into masculine and feminine which longed for each other.
Yes, this is my gift to you. Above ashes
On a bitter, bitter earth. Above the subterranean
Echo of clamorings and vows. So that now at dawn
You must be attentive: the tilt of a head,
A hand with a comb, two faces in a mirror
Are only forever once, even if unremembered,
So that you watch what is, though it fades away,
And are grateful every moment for your being.
Let that little park with greenish marble busts
In the pearl-gray light, under a summer drizzle,
Remain as it was when you opened the-gate.
And the street of tall peeling porticoes
Which this love of yours suddenly transformed.

CZESLAW MILOSZ
Translated by the author and Robert Haas

On the Road

Our roof was grapes and the broad hands of the vine
as we two drank in the vine-chinky shade
of harvest France;
and wherever the white road led we could not care,
it had brought us there
to the arbour built on a valley side where time,
if time any more existed, was that river
of so profound a current, it at once
both flowed and stayed.

We two. And nothing in the whole world was lacking.
It is later one realizes. I forget
the exact year or what we said. But the place
for a lifetime glows with noon. There are the rustic
table and the benches set; beyond the river
forests as soft as fallen clouds, and in
our wine and eyes I remember other noons.
It is a lot to say, nothing was lacking;
river, sun and leaves, and I am making
words to say 'grapes' and 'her skin'.

BERNARD SPENCER

The Good Morrow

I wonder, by my troth, what thou and I
    Did, till we loved? Were we not weaned till then,
But sucked on country pleasures, childishly?
    Or snorted we in the seven sleepers' den?
    'Twas so; but this, all pleasures fancies be.
    If ever any beauty I did see,
Which I desired, and got, 'twas but a dream of thee.

And now good morrow to our waking souls,
    Which watch not one another out of fear;
For love, all love of other sights controls,
    And makes one little room, an every where.
Let sea-discoverers to new worlds have gone,
    Let maps to others, worlds on worlds have shown:
Let us possess one world, each hath one, and is one.

My face in thine eye, thine in mine appears,
    And true plain hearts do in the faces rest:
Where can we find two better hemispheres
    Without sharp north, without declining west?
Whatever dies, was not mixed equally;
    If our two loves be one, or, thou and I
Love so alike that none do slacken, none can die.

JOHN DONNE

Song

Two doves upon the selfsame branch,
   Two lilies on a single stem,
Two butterflies upon one flower: –
   Oh happy they who look on them!

Who look upon them hand in hand
   Flushed in the rosy summer light;
Who look upon them hand in hand,
   And never give a thought to night.

CHRISTINA ROSSETTI

'i carry your heart with me
(i carry it in my heart)'

i carry your heart with me(i carry it in
my heart) i am never without it(anywhere
i go you go, my dear and whatever is done
by only me is your doing,my darling)
                                    i fear;
no fate(for you are my fate, my sweet)i want
no world(for beautiful you are my world,my true)
and it's you are whatever a moon has always meant
and whatever a sun will always sing is you

here is the deepest secret nobody knows
(here is the root of the root and the bud of the bud
and the sky of the sky of a tree called life;which grows
higher than soul can hope or mind can hide)
and this is the wonder that's keeping the stars apart

i carry your heart(i carry it in my heart)

E. E. CUMMINGS

The Confirmation

Yes, yours, my love, is the right human face.
I in my mind had waited for this long,
Seeing the false and searching for the true,
Then found you as a traveller finds a place
Of welcome suddenly amid the wrong
Valleys and rocks and twisting roads. But you,
What shall I call you? A fountain in a waste,
A well of water in a country dry,
Or anything that's honest and good, an eye
That makes the whole world bright. Your open heart,
Simple with giving, gives the primal deed,
The first good world, the blossom, the blowing seed,
The hearth, the steadfast land, the wandering sea.
Not beautiful or rare in every part.
But like yourself, as they were meant to be.

EDWIN MUIR

154

To My Dear and Loving Husband

If ever two were one, then surely we.
If ever man were loved by wife, then thee;
If ever wife was happy in a man,
Compare with me ye women if you can
I prize thy love more than whole mines of gold,
Or all the riches that the East doth hold.
My love is such that rivers cannot quench,
Nor ought but love from thee give recompense.
Thy love is such I can no way repay;
The heavens reward thee manifold, I pray,
Then while we live, in love let's so persever,
That when we live no more we may live ever.

ANNE BRADSTREET

Epithalamium

Ask not, this night, how we shall love
When we are three-year lovers;
How clothes, as lapsing tides, as love,
May slide, three summers over;
Nor ask when the eye's quick darknesses
Throw shadows on our skin
How we shall know our nakedness
In the difference of things.

Ask not whose salty hand turns back
The sea's sheet on the shore,
Or how the spilt and broken moon rides
Still each wave's humped back –
Ask not, for it is given as my pledge
That night shall be our sole inquisitor,
Day our respondent, and each parting as the bride
And groom, an hour before their marriage.

ELIZABETH GARRETT

For a Wedding

Cousin, I think the shape of a marriage
is like the shelves my parents have carried
through Scotland to London, three houses;

is not distinguished, fine, French-polished,
but plywood and tatty, made
in the first place for children to batter,

still carrying markings in green felt-tip,
but always, where there are books
and a landing, managing to fit;

that marriage has lumps like
their button-backed sofa, constantly,
shortly, about to be stuffed;

and that love grows fat
as their squinting cat, swelling
round as a loaf from her basket.

I wish you years that shape, that form,
and a pond in a Sunday, urban garden;
where you'll see your joined reflection tremble,

stand and watch the waterboatmen
skate with ease across the surface tension.

KATE CLANCHY

White Writing

No vows written to wed you,
I write them white,
my lips on yours,
light in the soft hours of our married years.

No prayers written to bless you,
I write them white,
your soul a flame,
bright in the window of your maiden name.

No laws written to guard you,
I write them white,
your hand in mine,
palm against palm, lifeline, heartline.

No rules written to guide you,
I write them white,
words on the wind,
traced with a stick where we walk on the sand.

No news written to tell you,
I write it white,
foam on a wave
as we lift up our skirts in the sea, wade,

see last gold sun behind clouds,
inked water in moonlight.
No poems written to praise you,
I write them white.

CAROL ANN DUFFY

Wedding

From time to time our love is like a sail
and when the sail begins to alternate
from tack to tack, it's like a swallowtail
and when the swallow flies it's like a coat;
and if the coat is yours, it has a tear
like a wide mouth and when the mouth begins
to draw the wind, it's like a trumpeter
and when the trumpet blows, it blows like millions . . .
and this, my love, when millions come and go
beyond the need of us, is like a trick;
and when the trick begins, it's like a toe
tip-toeing on a rope, which is like luck;
and when the luck begins, it's like a wedding,
which is like love, which is like everything.

ALICE OSWALD

from The Wife of Bath's Tale

And whan the knyght saugh verraily al this,
That she so fair was, and so yong there-to,
For joye he hente hir in his armes two,
His herte bathed in a bath of blisse.
A thousand tyme a-newe he gan hir kisse,
And she obeyed hym in every thing
That myghte doon hym plesance or likyng.

And thus they live unto hir lyves ende
In parfit joye; and Jhesu Crist us sende
Housbondes meeke, yonge, and fressh a-bedde,
And grace t'overbyde hem that we wedde;
And eek I praye Jhesu shorte hir lyves
That wol nat be governed by hir wyves;
And olde and angry nygardes of dispence,
God sende hem soone verray pestilence!

GEOFFREY CHAUCER

Marriage Song

I

It was that dressing-gown, deep medieval blue
and starred with tiny flowers, that did for me.
Hair up, fresh from the bath, you stood there
like a book of hours. It was a charity

in me to take confession of those breasts
and rosy nipples, of the clasping root
that split old grimy London head to foot,
and nail the clamour of your lips. Alas!

I am of them that snuffle up small print
and range the world in transubstantial books
which armours me against small deaths but not,
it seems, this odyssey of killing looks.

II

In Hampstead, on the tilt, repeating word
for word our promptings, looking up to see
the solemn paradigms, a family
which mingled hope and pain as something stirred
and broke the surface of them all, we said
the word and walked out smiling. Photographs
snatched by a friend showed later that you'd cried
at first, balancing the bride

in you against the funeral of a girl
who'd left blood on the landscape, run amok
to lock out accidentals. It took
two continents to grow you: now you move
into the narrow orbit of sheer love
high up above them all, where comets shine
and men rehearse quotations, all space-time
bent round in adoration: now we cut
and cast the skin we lived in, as the moon comes up.

WILLIAM SCAMMELL

They Are a Tableau at the Kissing-Gate

Maids of honour, bridegroom, bride,
the best man in a grey silk suit,
a flash to catch them in the arching
stone, confettied by a sudden gust –
an apple-tree in full white spread
beyond the reach of bone and dust.

I am the driver in a passing car:
the wedding-dress a cloud of lace.
A small hand clutching at a skirt,
some nervous bridesmaid, eight
or maybe nine years old, has seen
the blossom fall, has closed her eyes –

her head falls back into the scent,
the soundless whirr and whirl of earth-
bound petals, like sycamore seeds
on a current of air, silent helicopters
bringing light – a wedding-gift
the bride will brush away, unconsciously.

This is no ordinary act, no summer fête,
another simple wedding held in June.
This is the wind shaking the apple-tree,
the bell above the kissing-gate,
the sudden fall of blossom into light
which only love and innocence can see.

We must be held accountable to love:
where they step out together arm in arm
as newly-weds, spring-cleaned, and climb
into a waiting car beneath a summer sky,
the blossom will still fall, unstoppable –
a drift of change across a changeless time.

JANE HOLLAND

from *Paradise Lost*

'". . . I now see
Bone of my bone, flesh of my flesh, my self
Before me; woman is her name, of man
Extracted; for this cause he shall forgo
Father and mother, and to his wife adhere,
And they shall be one flesh, one heart, one soul."
  'She heard me thus, and, though divinely brought,
Yet innocence and virgin modesty
Her virtue and the conscience of her worth,
That would be wooed, and not unsought be won,
Not obvious, not obtrusive, but retired,
The more desirable – or, to say all,
Nature herself, though pure of sinful thought –
Wrought in her so, that seeing me, she turned;
I followed her; she what was honour knew,
And with obsequious majesty approved
My pleaded reason. To the nuptial bower
I led her blushing like the morn; all heaven,
And happy constellations, on that hour
Shed their selectest influence; the earth
Gave sign of gratulation, and each hill;
Joyous the birds; fresh gales and gentle airs
Whispered it to the woods, and from their wings
Flung rose, flung odours from the spicy shrub,

Disporting, till the amorous bird o' night
Sung spousal, and bid haste the evening star
On his hill-top to light the bridal lamp.'

JOHN MILTON

Jewish Wedding Song

The season for paradox has come
when two become one,
yet remain distinctive,

when our little enclave
overflows with reminiscences
and a din of happy wishes

and we bask in familiar voices,
and all is blessed friendliness.
The complex self now is suspended,

for this is a day for a rondo,
a jig, a romp . . . whatever,
a day for anecdotes and toasts,

when the best man
rises with a roguish smile
and holds his glass high:

'Here's to Bacchus,' he calls out,
'that outsider, that *goy*,'
and the young men laugh

and stomp their feet.
And so it goes the rounds.
Even the elders dance.

Let elixir fall now from the air
and a circle of humming-birds
hover over your heads

as you pledge to be steadfast
and generous to each other,
and the cantor sings a song of songs.

Do you not hear the ancient voice
of Israel calling
for kindness and responsibility?

Night falls, alas
and the rondo comes to an end
and vanishes into memory.

The musicians have departed
and paradox is asleep.

May the wisdom of Solomon
be with you.

CARL RAKOSI

Insular Sounds

Because sea in a seashell
comes to a standstill,

the sleepless, innumerable
peals of a seagull

soon are inaudible
in all but a seashell.

And from soupcan to soupcan
a string of our secrets

we swept as small boys
from seashore to sea-wall

loops through the bones
of such washed-up debris

as a cockleshell in shingle
which recovers at an angle

hymns no longer sung
by an island congregation.

You can hear the sound of confetti
fall on my brother's shoulder.

You can hear a beaten-up engine
driving away from the altar,

the sound of soupcans and seashells
tenderly lashed to the fender.

JOHN REDMOND

The Owl and the Pussy-Cat

The Owl and the Pussy-Cat went to sea
    In a beautiful pea-green boat.
They took some honey, and plenty of money
    Wrapped up in a five-pound note.
The Owl looked up to the stars above,
    And sang to a small guitar,
'O lovely Pussy! O Pussy, my love,
What a beautiful Pussy you are,
      You are,
      You are!
What a beautiful Pussy you are!'

Pussy said to the Owl, 'You elegant fowl!
    How charmingly sweet you sing!
O let us be married! too long we have tarried:
    But what shall we do for a ring?'
They sailed away, for a year and a day,
    To the land where the Bong-Tree grows,
And there in a wood a Piggy-wig stood,
With a ring at the end of his nose,
      His nose,
      His nose!
With a ring at the end of his nose.

'Dear Pig, are you willing to sell for one shilling
    Your ring?' Said the Piggy, 'I will.'
So they took it away, and were married next day
    By the Turkey who lives on the hill.

They dinèd on mince, and slices of quince,
    Which they ate with a runcible spoon;
And hand in hand, on the edge of the sand
    They danced by the light of the moon,
        The moon,
        The moon,
They danced by the light of the moon.

EDWARD LEAR

Match

Love has not made us good.
We still do all the cynics said we would –
Struggle like heroes searching for a war,
Still want too much, and more.

Love has not made us nice.
Elders and betters with their best advice
Can't stir us from the lounger by the pool.
We dodge all work like school,

Leave urgent debts unpaid,
Cancel the solemn promises we've made
If loyalties or circumstances change.
Our thoughts are no less strange,

But love has made us last.
We do together all that in the past
We did alone; err not as one but two
And this is how I knew.

SOPHIE HANNAH

Love (III)

Love bade me welcome; yet my soul drew back,
      Guilty of dust and sin.
But quick-eyed love, observing me grow slack
      From my first entrance in,
Drew nearer to me, sweetly questioning
      If I lacked anything.

A guest, I answered, worthy to be here:
      Love said, 'You shall be he.'
I the unkind, ungrateful? 'Ah my dear,
      I cannot look on thee.'
Love took my hand, and smiling did reply,
      'Who made the eyes but I?'

'Truth Lord, but I have marred them: let my shame
      Go where it doth deserve.'
'And know you not,' says love, 'who bore the blame?'
      'My dear, then I will serve.'
'You must sit down,' says love, 'and taste my meat':
      So I did sit and eat.

GEORGE HERBERT

from Song of the Open Road

Listen! I will be honest with you,
I do not offer the old smooth prizes, but offer rough new
  prizes,
These are the days that must happen to you:
You shall not heap up what is called riches,
You shall scatter with lavish hand all that you earn or
  achieve . . .

Allons! After the great Companions, and to belong to
  them!
They too are on the road – they are the swift and majestic
  men –
                          they are the greatest women,
Enjoyers of calm seas and storms of seas,
Sailors of many a ship, walkers of many a mile of land,
Habitués of many distant countries, habitués of far-distant
  dwellings,
Trusters of men and women, observers of cities, solitary
  toilers,
Pausers and contemplators of tufts, blossoms, shells of the
  shore,
Dancers at wedding-dances, kissers of brides, tender
  helpers of children,
                          bearers of children . . .

Camerado, I give you my hand!
I give you my love more precious than money,

I give you myself before preaching or law;
Will you give me yourself? will you come travel with me?
Shall we stick by each other as long as we live?

WALT WHITMAN

True Ways of Knowing

Not an ounce excessive, not an inch too little,
Our easy reciprocations. You let me know
The way a boat would feel, if it could feel,
The intimate support of water.

The news you bring me has been news forever,
So that I understand what a stone would say
If only a stone could speak. Is it sad a grassblade
Can't know how it is lovely?

Is it sad that you can't know, except by hearsay
(My gossiping failing words) that you are the way
A water is that can clench its palm and crumple
A boat's confiding timbers?

But that's excessive, and too little. Knowing
The way a circle would describe its roundness,
We touch two selves and feel, complete and gentle,
The intimate support of being.

The way that flight would feel a bird flying
(If it could feel) is the way a space that's in
A stone that's in a water would know itself
If it had our way of knowing.

NORMAN MACCAIG

Primitive

I have heard about the civilised,
the marriages run on talk, elegant and
honest, rational. But you and I
are savages. You come in with a bag,
hold it out to me in silence.
I know Moo Shu Pork when I smell it
and understand the message: I have
pleased you greatly last night. We sit
quietly, side by side, to eat,
the long pancakes dangling and spilling,
fragrant sauce dripping out,
and glance at each other askance, wordless,
the corners of our eyes clear as spear points
laid along the sill to show
a friend sits with a friend here.

SHARON OLDS

Husband to Wife: Party-Going

Turn where the stairs bend
In this house; statued in other light,
Allow the host to ease you from your coat.
Stand where the stairs bend,
A formal distance from me, then descend
With delicacy conscious but not false
And take my arm, as if I were someone else.

Tonight, in a strange room
We will be strangers: let our eyes be blind
To all our customary stances –
Remark how well I'm groomed,
I will explore your subtly-voiced nuances
Where delicacy is conscious but not false,
And take your hand, as if you were someone else.

Home forgotten, rediscover
Among chirruping of voices, chink of glass,
Those simple needs that turned us into lovers,
How solitary was the wilderness
Until we met, took leave of hosts and guests,
And with delicate consciousness of what was false
Walked off together, as if there were no one else.

BRIAN JONES

Atlas

There is a kind of love called maintenance,
Which stores the WD40 and knows when to use it;

Which checks the insurance, and doesn't forget
The milkman; which remembers to plant bulbs;

Which answers letters; which knows the way
The money goes; which deals with dentists

And Road Fund Tax and meeting trains,
And postcards to the lonely; which upholds

The permanently ricketty elaborate
Structures of living; which is Atlas.

And maintenance is the sensible side of love,
Which knows what time and weather are doing
To my brickwork; insulates my faulty wiring;
Laughs at my dryrotten jokes; remembers
My need for gloss and grouting; which keeps
My suspect edifice upright in air,
As Atlas did the sky.

U. A. FANTHORPE

Reflecting on Old Age

We are as light as wood ash, dense as stone.
Our muscles come to know the weight of bone,
The sensual happiness of lying down.
A little milk the gradual years have pressed
Into our eyes that easily over-run.
Our vague hair is as volatile as dust.

Waking and sleep are mutual, so far on
In marriage that we speak of one alone,
Sleep without waking, as in a foreign tongue
Stumbling on consonants. Against the dark,
Coeval kindness, beneficence of the young
With our time's cares cross in a lattice-work.

Honey of small events, of passing states
We take – as when a light flame oscillates
In the smokeless coal. In the winter grate's
Rock garden it blows, translucent as a wild
Flower, as woodsorrel; or a bird's heart, it beats;
And gives peace, as if worlds were reconciled.

On the railway bank not only bracken, once,
I remember, but the dying grass was bronze
In transverse light; and beyond the journey, friends.
Happiness even passing imagination,
Foretold by straws of grass and bracken fronds,
Late in the day, their welcome at the station.

Too hard in age to trawl the heavy seas.
I settle for summations, instances,
Remembering (in time's interstices)
Time taken to sit in the tropic after-sun
In an open gallery, in hands cup or glass,
With two or three; here now, by a fire, with one.

E. J. SCOVELL

from *Paradise Lost*

Two of far nobler shape, erect and tall,
God-like erect, with native honour clad
In naked majesty, seemed lords of all,
And worthy seemed; for in their looks divine
The image of their glorious maker shone,
Truth, wisdom, sanctitude severe and pure –
Severe, but in true filial freedom placed,
Whence true authority in men: though both
Not equal, as their sex not equal seemed;
For contemplation he and valour formed,
For softness she and sweet attractive grace;
He for God only, she for God in him;
His fair large front and eye sublime declared
Absolute rule; and hyacinthine locks
Round from his parted forelock manly hung
Clustering, but not beneath his shoulders broad:
She as a veil down to the slender waist,
Her unadornèd golden tresses wore
Dishevelled, but in wanton ringlets waved
As the vine curls her tendrils – which implied
Subjection, but required with gentle sway,
And by her yielded, by him best received
Yielded, with coy submission, modest pride,
And sweet reluctant amorous delay.
Nor those mysterious parts were then concealed;
Then was not guilty shame, dishonest shame
Of nature's works, honour dishonourable,
Sin-bred, how have ye troubled all mankind

With shows instead, mere shows of seeming pure,
And banished from man's life his happiest life,
Simplicity and spotless innocence.
So passed they naked on, nor shunned the sight
Of God or angel, for they thought no ill:
So hand in hand they passed, the liveliest pair
That ever since in love's embraces met –
Adam the goodliest man of men since born
His sons; the fairest of her daughters Eve.

JOHN MILTON

Index of Authors and Translators

Index of Titles and First Lines

extracts reading groups

competitions books new

discounts extracts

competitions extracts

books new discounts

new events reading groups

events books extracts

new extracts events

new titles reading groups

interviews

reading groups events extracts new

discounts books

new books events

events new events

discounts extracts discounts

www.panmacmillan.com

extracts events reading groups

competitions books extracts new